MW01705158

Your Words, Your Story

Cynthia Harrison

TAM Press

2007

"Musical Notes & Lofty Theories" originally appeared in Room of One's Own, Vancouver, BC; "Cherry Vanilla" in the Journal of the Division of Letters: Marygrove College, Detroit, Michigan.

TCAM Press is a creative writing resource for short story, novel, memoir, screenplay, children's stories and poetry as well as how to publish.

Ordering Information: Contact TCAM Press, 45479 Spagnuolo, Macomb, Michigan 48044 or request purchasing information from TCAM press@gmail.com.

Library of Congress Number: 2007907986

ISBN: 9780615161556

Printed by: Sheridan Books, Inc. Inc Ann Arbor, Michigan

www.sheridanbooks.com

Cover photography by Debra Bressman, cover design and logo by Bdazzled Designs, L.L.C.

For Al
My husband, who loves the writer part of me
along with all the other bits.

For Mike
My son, who created and
manages my website.

For Tim
My son, who put the
T in TCAM.

I love you guys.

Contents

Preface

All creative writing uses the same set of skills. It doesn't matter if you want to write narrative poetry, memoir, short stories, children's literature, novels, or screenplays. They all have common elements.

Not everyone who takes my class wants to write the same kind of story. So what I've done is talk about the types of stories my students have been most interested in pursuing. Luckily, I've had experience writing in all these areas, and I've used examples of my own writing to illustrate the skills I talk about.

We'll work from the beginning forward: from the first things you need to know, up to more advanced skills of greater complexity. I explain the skill sets in chapters structured around each type of creative writing. So even if you're writing a novel, not a screenplay, you'll learn important information in the screenplay chapter.

My own creative chronology kicks off each chapter. You get mini-memoirs of my own checkered writing history, as well as some of my actual poetry and stories, published and unpublished, as examples.

To be a better writer, you should master all of the skills this text covers, then use them or not, as you prefer. As the saying goes, know the rules before you break them. My exercises go from basic to complex. You master skills by practicing them, so, to get the most out of this book, read it from beginning to end, and work on all of the exercises, even if you're writing children's lit and not memoir.

Finally, if an exercise takes you away from my directions, flow with it. That's why it's called Creative Writing and not Writing By Numbers.

ONE

Every Story

"Writers will often find themselves steering by stars that are disturbingly in motion."

E. B. White

Hollywood Hook

Three days ago, I flew home from a meeting in Los Angeles with a literary agent who loves my novel. Twenty-five years ago, I was a creative writing student who didn't know the first thing about what makes a story work. I knew how to write, and I'd even published poetry and book reviews. But my heart's desire was to tell stories.

What I didn't know then, but have since figured out, is that, for me, anyway, it's all story. Memoir, poetry, fiction, and screenplay all tell stories, or, in the case of non-narrative poetry, at least help develop the descriptive qualities important for a writer of stories. The best of these various kinds of writing all have common story elements. It took me 25 years to figure this out, but all of the forms of writing I've practiced support each other in interesting ways. My writing journey has been perfect for my own special learning. It's gotten me where I am today, writing this book you hold in your hands or read on your screen.

The Basics

Whatever kind of writing you want to do, you all need to practice the same basic skills: grammar, diction, character, setting, plot, pacing, and conflict. Impeccable grammar and precise diction are the ground on which character, setting, plot, pacing and conflict are built. I'm going to assume you've got a good grasp of grammar and diction, or if you don't, you're willing to learn as you go. What I want to teach you is how to tell a story, and every story, including narrative poetry, memoir, fiction, and screenplay, begins with character.

Character

In my early writing experiences, my characters tended to start with me, or some version of myself. In memoir, the character is, of course, me, or at least the part of me I'm presenting to the world. In fiction, sometimes my characters diverge wildly from who I truly am, and sometimes they're so familiar they could almost be me.

As I grew as a writer and aged as a person, I became less interested in writing yet another version of myself and more intrigued by creating characters completely from my imagination. I found it stimulating to figure out what it would feel like to be this person. I had to image them so deeply that, at least for the time I was writing the words, I became that character.

Your experience may differ, but if you don't know where to begin building a character, starting with yourself is as good a way as any to go.

Setting

The world characters inhabit is part of them, helps make them who they are. Setting includes not just time and place but gesture, furniture, and the circumstances of the character's life. In story, setting and character intertwine. No character lives in a vacuum; where they live and how they live is part of who they are.

Plot, Pacing & Conflict

Plot needs conflict to survive. Pacing refers to the writer's choices about how much of the conflict to reveal and when to do so. Television shows like 24 are fast-paced, with almost constant action. But even Jack Bauer gets a minute or two a day to close his eyes, to sit down and rest. Conflict helps propel the plot. It needs to come from deep within the character, from a blocked goal, hidden motive, secret wish, or all three. Conflict needs to come fully alive on the page. It needs to be, most of the time, active.

A Conflicted Start

I am not fond of conflict in life, so I tend to avoid it on the page, which used to make my stories sort of uneventful. When I deliberately began trying to insert conflict into my opening scenes, it was awkward. For example, I started one story with a Ninja fight, which I was sure would be dazzling, undeniable conflict.

Imagine several suburban couples, mid-thirties, on the patio drinking beer and wine on a summer evening when a group of black-clad punks appear out of the night and commences beating the crap out of everyone.

My thinking process: *If there's a big huge fight, that's conflict. Right?*

Maybe, but who cares? Too many fists and no human motive are puzzling, not moving. Readers need a reason to care. And that comes from imagining a character, or several characters, and putting them in a true setting, and seeing what happens. Conflict arises naturally from story. Well, story and a good antagonist.

In mainstream stories, the central character, aka protagonist, aka you if you're writing memoir, has a goal. The antagonist blocks that goal. This simple recipe, if used correctly, moves story at a pace that compels readers to turn pages.

Exercise 1: Ink Warmer

Maybe you know exactly what you want to write and just need to know HOW. Or, maybe you love writing in general but want to find out specifically what kind of writing you should pursue. Whatever you want to write, these questions should help form specific goals.

This ink warmer is a first chance for you to switch from critical to creative mode. Don't worry about wording. Go with first thoughts. Write quickly and with confidence.

1. What section of the newspaper do you read first?

2. What television programs do you watch?

3. If you had a weblog, what would your subject be?

4. What kind of movies do you like? Name the last three movies you saw and loved.

5. What magazines do you read? What feature or column do you turn to first?

6. When you visit a bookstore or library, what section do you check out first? List your five favorite books.

7. If you were offered a good salary to write anything, what would you write?

8. What common themes appear in your above responses? These themes are the ones you most want to explore.

The Writing Habit

I write every morning, first thing, because it's my golden time, the time of day when my mind works best, when I feel happiest, when I'm most inclined to indulge myself. Even if I'm not working on anything in particular, I sit down at my desk or more often in my cozy chair, with pen and paper and just allow the thoughts to flow from my head to my heart to my fingers to the page. I love to write, so I allow myself the daily pleasure of doing what I love.

Like any habit, it takes a while to develop a daily writing practice. For the duration of this course, make that your homework. Each day, set a timer for 10 or 20 minutes, and write whatever comes to you without any critical interference. Just let it flow. Or creak. Or list. Whatever writing wants to come out let it come. If nothing comes, write a letter to yourself in which you try to understand why you want to write, what you want to write about, how you think you might go about it once you're ready to begin. In other words, interview yourself.

Use a computer or pen and paper. Work on something for class or just jot thoughts in a journal entry. What you write is completely up to you. Establishing a habitual routine is the only goal. And this is required because you love to write and you deserve to do what you love every day. Also, it helps if you can figure out your golden time, and write then.

When I was younger, I didn't have as much free time as I have now. I had flirting to do, parties to attend, and hell to raise. Later, as a direct result of the flirting and partying, I raised children instead of hell. Then, as a single mom, I went to college. All of this stuff takes time.

So I know it's not easy to find your golden time and then use it for writing. If you're in the midst of growing a very full life, find 20 minutes a day, at any time of the day you can find those minutes, and use those minutes to write.

The more you write, the easier it gets, particularly if you give yourself permission to write terribly. Who cares? Nobody's going to read the words except you, unless you decide later that this or that string of words is pretty good, and you turn them into a story. For now, keep your writing in a notebook that you file away and forget when the rest of your life calls.

Later, reread your notebook. You'll find hidden gems and wonder, *Did I really write that?*

Getting started is the hardest part for people who don't yet have the daily writing habit, which is why you should not overthink or censor yourself. Allow yourself to draft something terrible, something that breaks every grammar rule in the known universe. Once you shut off the internal critic, the words tend to flow.

First drafts can be revised later. But to get that first draft, you have to forget later and be in the now. If you're like me, you'll also have to remind yourself over and over again than it's okay to write terribly today.

Event or Meaning?

Writer Jane Smiley says that every writer is an "event" or a "meaning" type of writer. There is no quality difference, just a preference for one style of writing over another. Given your replies to my questions, you should now have a few clues about which kind of writer you are. If you prefer action films, you're probably an "event" writer. If you religiously watch the Independent Film Channel, you are likely a "meaning" kind of writer.

Is the sports page what you look for after scanning the front page headlines of the newspaper? Event. Or do you go right for the Lifestyle section? Meaning.

Do you prefer music or lyrics? Music's more event and lyrics hold meaning.

Finding out what kind of writer you are, or where you fall on the spectrum, because most writers care about both event and meaning, can be time-efficient. If you know what kind of writer you are, you won't waste time trying to write what you don't love or are not designed to do. And writing for any reason other than because you love the process always shows on the page.

Exercise 2: Event or Meaning?

Write a paragraph or a page describing why you believe you are an "event" or "meaning" writer. After you're finished we'll read these out loud. So-meaning or event? Or a bit of both?

TWO

Poetry

"If you want what the syllables want,

just do your job."

Charles Wright

High School Outsider

In 1969, I was popular and perky, the star reporter for my junior high school newspaper, *The Cardinal.* My journalism teacher, Mrs. Grow, taught the most vital writing lesson of all: to believe in my talent. Then I started high school, and things changed; I changed. About the only thing that stayed the same is that I knew I was a writer.

In high school, I gave up the journalism crowd and acquired a whole new group of friends, most of whom were outsider types like me. The thing that made me feel so different was this secret I carried: I thought I was the only living poet. All the poets we studied in English class were dead. I was the only person I knew who wrote poetry.

Like a lot of teenagers, I loved music. I noticed the lyrics more than the guitars and drums. Most of my friends looked at me funny when I quoted lyrics. They just liked the bass riff or the great guitar solo.

I wasn't writing rhyming love poems, like the ones I'd published in The Cardinal on Valentine's Day. No, like my mood, my poems were angry, dark. I poured my sadness and bewilderment onto the page. It saved my life.

I didn't know it at the time, but my case was not unusual; many teenagers use poetry to cope with scary emotions. Along my rocky way, as I scribbled my lines in notebooks I never showed to anyone, I acquired an enhanced sense of the rhythm of words.

Later, when I moved from poetry to prose, I already knew how to make a sentence sing. Couldn't plot my way out of a spiral notebook, but that's getting ahead of myself.

Curiosity

My favorite poetry and song lyrics are narrative. They tell a story. Here's my secret to writing a great narrative poem: you have to be curious. Curiosity is vital for a writer. You have to be interested in who and what you're writing about in order for the reader to be interested in what you have to say. You do this by being honestly interested in people and life.

You also need to be intrigued by the way the words interplay on the page, or in the song. Do this by reading your poem aloud and listening to how it sounds. Collect words that comfort your ears, or make them perk up, or create the exact kind of internal response your subject needs.

Exercise 3: The 5 Ws & the H

One of the first rules of journalism is to get the main facts: who, what, when, where, why and how. This works for narrative poems, too. Answer these six questions as fully as you can. If you don't know the answer to one or more of the questions, simply make something up. You can always change it later. If you want to write, but have no idea what story to tell, start with yourself or another interesting person, real or imaginary, and answer the questions that way.

Depicting Emotional Territory

Poetry is compressed language often depicting emotional territory. Writing poetry increases descriptive powers. Poetry can be formal or informal, rhymed or free verse, intensely symbolic or plainly spoken. Most contemporary poetry mixes more formal elements, when used at all, with free verse.

Poems generally have a speaker who addresses a particular audience, not necessarily the reader. For example a love poem most often speaks to the beloved, not the reader. Poetry compresses image and/or emotion using figurative language and other poetic devices into lyric, narrative, and other forms.

Practicing writing poetry can help all writers, not just poets, develop a distinctive voice because of the deep attention paid to what language can do.

Developing Character via Poetry

Most people, including fictional people, have a set of characteristics, personality traits that harmonize with each other. For example, a nervous person will exhibit certain behaviors: fidgeting, sweating, frowning, trembling. A perfectionist will become nervous and thus exhibit these behaviors if things are not perfect. Insecurity is said to be at the base of perfectionism, and this insecurity only increases when a perfectionist meets someone who has no patience for people who take too long to accomplish a task because they want to get it exactly right.

The three traits that go together then are anxiety, perfectionism and insecurity. The trait that opposes perfectionism is impatience. An impatient person is likely an anxious person, too. However, their anxiety often manifests as anger rather than nervousness.

Complex characters in narrative poems have many traits that seem to go together, but what makes them really interesting is their paradoxical trait. The thing about them that doesn't match the other things.

"Richard Cory" author Edwin Arlington Robinson (1869-1935) uses this character paradox as a twist at the end of his famous poem.

Richard Cory

Whenever Richard Cory went down town,
We people on the pavement looked at him:
He was a gentleman from sole to crown,
Clean-favoured and imperially slim.

And he was always quietly arrayed,
And he was always human when he talked;
But still he fluttered pulses when he said,
"Good Morning!" and he glittered when he walked.

And he was rich, yes, richer than a king,
And admirably schooled in every grace:
In fine -- we thought that he was everything
To make us wish that we were in his place.

So on we worked and waited for the light,
And went without the meat and cursed the bread,
And Richard Cory, one calm summer night,
Went home and put a bullet in his head.

What are Richard Cory's basic characteristics?

What's the paradox?

In Robinson's time, end-rhymed, formally measured poetry, with lines of similar length and sound, was popular. Contemporary poets, if they employ rhyme at all, use internal rhyme, alliteration, or other subtle forms. Free verse is less formally structured, as well. Here's a contemporary character poem I wrote a really long time ago.

Somewhere in America

Somewhere in America, there is a woman
Searching for happiness in the pages of
J. C. Penney:

Have you found yourself yet?
Where do you fit among the wicker
& the glass?
Would you really be fine
If you could sleep on satin?

I know you.
With your love affairs every afternoon
On channels 2, 4, and 7.
Your jeans are tight.
So is your life.

Your gallon jars of guilt
Crowd the cabinets.
Break them out
Paint the cellar with them
Throw the empties away.

What are the basic characteristics of this American woman?

What's her paradox?

Exercise 4: Character Poem

Create a character poem in rhyme or free verse. Describe a character: you, someone you know, someone you invent. Give this character three consistent core characteristics and a paradox. Use your 5Ws & H as a starting point if you want to.

THREE

Memoir

"She was real, but she was also imaginary."

Paul Auster

Death of the Only Living Poet

There were only four dry days in June the year my basement flooded. Elvis hadn't died yet, but another, more personal loss was happening right under my feet.

The morning started out like any other. I got up before my husband left for work to make coffee in our new stainless steel pot. As a young bride, I was proud of my stuff and spent several hours a day keeping everything, including the coffee pot, shiny and clean.

As I listened for the shower to turn off, Maxwell House grounds spilled onto the counter. I grabbed a dish cloth and wiped the mess away before it could stain the grout between the tiny ceramic tiles. When the shower stopped running, I turned on the radio.

Mike liked jazz, so I only listened to two songs before he came out. At least they were good ones. "Dreams" by Fleetwood Mac and "Running on Empty" by stone fox Jackson Brown.

Mike looked a little like Jackson Brown. He had the same full lips and the straight shiny hair. He kissed me at the front door. He was carrying a briefcase, not a guitar, which was fine with me. I'd dated more loser musicians than I liked to remember.

"Pork chops," Mike said, a normal happy husband giving his wife instructions for dinner. I stood there at the door, watching his car roll down the wet road. I was living the best dream of my life. My last boyfriend, John, had been a vegetarian who didn't smoke and didn't allow me to light up in his house. Mike and I had ashtrays in every room. John hadn't wanted to get married or have kids, either, and even though he was a musician, he'd never once asked to read my poems.

I turned away from the rainy day and picked up the novel I'd finished yesterday, turning to the back of the book where the author had inserted a series of love poems. I had never read poems like these. Unrhymed. Profane. Gorgeously sexual. For years, I had believed I was the only living poet, the only sad, scared lonely girl who poured her heart onto the page.

But here was Erica Jong, doing it better, going deeper than I'd ever dreamed possible. Of course, I didn't write anymore. Once I'd fallen in love with the right guy, I lost the desire to plop my bleeding heart between the covers of a notebook. I put the novel down and went to start a load of laundry. Which was when I found out that sometime in the night the basement had flooded.

Even though he didn't like to be disturbed at work, I called Mike. Like a good knight, he promised to rescue me during his lunch hour.

"Okay, you can come down," Mike called up the stairs.

I popped the last bite of my peanut butter sandwich into my mouth and went to join my husband. The water that had reached halfway up the stairs was gone, although a mark midway up the cement walls showed where it had stood.

"Not in your bare feet!" Mike said. "Go wash them off and then come back down with shoes on. And bring your Playtex gloves."

"What?" I said, descending. "Why?"

He stopped sweeping puddles of water into the drain. He was so cute standing there in his rubber boots, one hand on the broom, one on his hip.

“Because this place is contaminated. That was sewer water. You’ll have to clean everything or throw it out.”

“Yuck,” I ran upstairs for my flip flops and came back down. He was sweeping again.

“Go through those boxes,” he indicated with a nod of his head, “and sterilize anything you want to keep.”

I saw the boxes full of stuff we hadn’t yet unpacked, stuff from our former lives that we hadn’t felt the need for now. With my yellow gloved hand I opened the first box. All Mike’s toys, little boy dump trucks and fire engines. Those could be saved for the son we planned to have someday. I moved the box aside with my foot.

“I’ve got to get back to work,” Mike said. “Do you have bleach? Lysol?”

I nodded, opening another box. My journals! I’d been writing diaries and filling notebooks with poems since I was 11 or 12. I saw right away that all three of the boxes were soaked, my stuff ruined. I grabbed the top notebook anyway. It was wet, but the ink had only smeared, not completely disappeared. Mike was already on his way up the stairs.

“My poems! Mike! What should I do?”

He looked back down at me, but I could tell he was already thinking about work again.

“Throw them away,” he said. And then he left.

He was right. I should just get rid of it all. I didn't write anymore, that had just been a phase. After ten years of recording my every agony, I'd come to a sweet resting place.

I kneeled over the boxes, not caring that I was wearing my favorite pair of bells. The jeans would survive; they were made of tough material. My writing, on the other hand, was disintegrating before my eyes. I pulled the top spiral bound books, which seemed semi-okay, out of the boxes. My oldest stuff--the white diary with gold lock and key, a picture of Mickey Dolenz, my favorite Monkee, hundreds of sheets of loose notebook paper—all of that was unsalvageable soup.

I came upstairs, my arms full of notebooks. I set them in the sink and then went back down, a jug of Lysol in one hand, old towels in the other.

I worked for hours, bagging up most of the stuff for Mike to throw out with the trash. I disinfected the walls, the hot water heater, the washer and dryer. I'd do the floor after Mike removed the garbage bags. After hanging damp cleaning rags over the clothesline that ran the length of the basement, I went upstairs to shower and start dinner.

I looked at my notebooks in the kitchen sink, and then noticed the light from outside shining down on them. For the first time in ten days, the sun had made it through the clouds. I opened all the windows before getting into the shower.

"What are these doing in here?" Mike said, coming home from work to a sink full of poems.

"Oh, I, ah, maybe I can save them." I combed out my long wet hair and avoided his eyes after I noticed that he was looking at me like I was crazy.

"Where's dinner?"

Mike only ate one meal a day, dinner. And he wanted it served the minute he walked in the door. I hadn't even defrosted the pork chops yet. And I was tired. I just wanted to sit on the sofa with a book.

"I worked all day in the basement! Let's go out." After spending years in the service industry waiting on other people, I loved being the customer. And Mike took me to really nice places, when he was in the mood.

"I'm tired. I work every day." He used a funny tone of voice, emphasizing the word *every*.

"Then I'll order pizza."

"Fine." He opened the fridge, got out a beer, and walked into the living room with it.

I called in the pizza order. I knew what he liked: pepperoni and cheese. I liked anything, so I was fine with getting his favorite. Maybe it would cheer him up. After I hung up the phone, I pulled the pork chops from the freezer and put them at the front of the refrigerator where I'd be sure to see them tomorrow.

While we waited for the pizza, Mike watched the news and I hung my poems up to dry like laundry on the line downstairs.

The next day, I set up a card table in one of the empty bedrooms. Then I called my mother and asked to borrow her typewriter. I went to the mall, but instead of shopping for shoes or another pair of velvet hot pants, I bought typing paper, a new ribbon, and a bottle of White Out.

Fifty-six poems survived the great flood of 1977. And surprising stuff happened when I typed them out. Hours flew by like minutes. I discovered the value in revision. And I also learned how to woo inspiration. The old seductress would come again.

True Stories

The story you've just read is true. I've been writing one version of it or another for many years, trying to get at the core of this turning point in my life as a writer. The first few times I wrote this piece, I changed the names and called it fiction, because the short story was in fashion. Now that memoir and personal essay are in vogue, the lines between fact and fiction have blurred into a hybrid called creative non-fiction.

In one sense, labels don't really matter. Story elements remain the same. On the other hand, if you plan to publish your story, it's important to be clear about whether what you've written is factual or embellished. James Frey learned this the hard way, in front of a national television audience, when he admitted to Oprah Winfrey that several of the so-called "facts" of his story were figments of his imagination.

Why did Frey exaggerate? Perhaps to heighten story elements, to increase tension, to further dramatize conflict. Certainly to make himself appear more heroic. When I heard that Frey first tried to sell *A Million Little Pieces* as fiction, it made sense. Writers have been adding drama to their true stories forever. It's a rite of passage also known as the "coming of age" story. Frey's mistake, other than the obvious one of wanting to be published so badly he'd lie, was in letting a memoir-hungry industry convince him that it was okay to blur the line between fact and fiction and go ahead and call it truth.

There's nothing wrong with tweaking true incidents. But, post-James Frey, the first rule of story should be to label any major tweakage fiction. One of the things *The Smoking Gun* website, first to break the story, called Frey on was turning a few hours in jail into a six-month stay. That's what I mean by "major tweakage."

In my story, I changed a few minor things. My husband was actually out of town when the flood happened, and my dad came over and rescued me. But those facts slowed down the real story about a turning point in my marriage and creative life. Collapsing three days into one didn't make me seem to suffer more. They didn't make my husband's character appear different. So, in my case, those details were fine to fix for a better structural flow and sharpened focus. They stay within the bounds of memoir, which is not exacting factual family history but more one member's memory of a specific time or event within the larger framework of a family's history.

Another thing I added that is not strictly "truth" is the pork chops. I can't remember what we had for dinner that night almost thirty years ago, but since my husband was a basic meat and potatoes man, and I tried hard to please him, pork chops could have been on the menu. Same with the specific songs on the radio. Details make a story come alive, and it's accepted in memoir to add these things where appropriate. You just have to be careful not to call yourself a movie star if you're a housewife from Michigan.

If your goal is to simply record the important moments of your life for family members, knowing the essential elements of story will help you shape your life into a dramatic structure, making it more interesting to read. So, when I say "story," you should read it to be truth OR fiction, whichever best suits your writing needs.

Point of View

Character is essential to story. Everything that happens rises from a central point of view character in whatever you write: short story, personal essay, memoir, screenplay, or novel. Focusing on your character and what she wants will add layers of complexity to your work.

In my story, the character is in the first person ("I") point of view. That is, everything that happens in the story is seen through the eyes of the "I" character. The other common stylistic point-of-view choice, particularly for fiction writers, is third person ("she" or "he").

In third-person limited omniscient everything in the story is seen from the perspective of one character at a time. This is a style choice, but seasoned writers don't "head-hop" or switch point of view without a good reason, because it confuses readers, takes them out of the story.

In a short piece, keeping to one point of view helps readers see the character as true. When using longer forms, like the novel or a screenplay, several characters' points of view are fine, as long as they're not all in the same paragraph. As a reader and critic, I admire the ability to sustain a single POV for an entire chapter, although as a writer, sometimes I change POV when I change scenes.

Finding the way into a character isn't difficult, but it takes time. Warm up exercises, where you just think about and discover things are great. Here are a whole bunch. They build on each other, so do them in order.

Exercise 5: 25 Things

Make a list of 25 things you love. Or hate. Or do a dozen of each.

Exercise 6: Sketch a Character

Give your character a name and three of the things from the list above. This character can be you, someone you know, or you can make this character up completely. Please don't use a character from another author's creative work, and this includes television characters and movie characters as well as fictional literary characters. Your character should be your own invention, someone who is not yet fully formed.

Exercise 7: Describe the World

After each of the three things your character loves, add one paragraph descriptions of whatever smells, sounds, words, images, or memories the things evoke for your character.

Exercise 8: Know Thy Character

Describe your character's physical appearance. You can be as vague or detailed as you like. You may not ever allude to any aspect of the physical description in the story, but you need to have a clear picture in your head.

Contemporary story tends to rely less on details of character appearance than earlier works, but again, it's a style thing. Maybe it's just my story that does not give visual cues about the main character. Maybe that's because it's in first person and how often do you think about how you look? Maybe when you look in the mirror. (And here's a hint: looking in a mirror to describe your first person character's features is a huge cliché. Avoid doing this. Also avoid having many people tell her how beautiful she is. That is just annoying.)

So why write it out if your character description may not end up in your story? Because you need to know all there is to know about this character. Whether details of the character's life, background, and appearance end up in the story or not, what you know about your character will inform how the character talks, acts, and thinks.

Remember, it's fine to make the character you. Just think about how you would look to others, and write that description down.

Exercise 9: Major Life Events

Using one side of the page and skipping plenty of lines between, make a list of 5-10 major events in your character's life (it's always fine to use your own life). You can do this in a number of ways: chronologically, as important events come to you, or grouped by subject, such as schools, birthdays, houses, boyfriends, or pets. You can make a list of "firsts." For example, first

bike ride

kiss

date

Chinese food

day of high school

apartment

child

job

On the other side of the page, write down the feelings each event evokes. Take your time with this part of the exercise. Sometimes feelings come in waves. If a major event is, for example, a death, the first feeling might be sadness. But underneath that could be anger, guilt, even relief, if the loved one had a long, painful illness. The point here is that if you link events or objects to feelings, it will make your story come alive.

Show and Tell

One of the most important things a writer learns is when to show and when to tell. In a story, you want to show emotional high moments in scene. "In scene" as opposed to summarizing just means looking through the character's eyes and describing what's happening as if you are there, what the characters do, feel, see, and say. Play these important moments out, beat by beat. Save summarization for the low moments. Writing this way will help readers invest in the emotional content of the story. Showing helps the reader feel what your character feels. This creates empathy and a willingness on the reader's part to follow the story to its end.

So how to "show" emotion? One way is to describe setting without any emotional attachment, and then discreetly, over time, begin to hint at the emotion held in the object. Here's an example of what I mean from "Death of the Only Living Poet":

As a young bride, I was proud of my stuff and spent several hours a day keeping everything, including the coffee pot, shiny and clean.

There's no negative emotional content yet. Everything seems perfectly fine.

As I listened for the shower to turn off, Maxwell House grounds spilled onto the counter. I grabbed a dish cloth and wiped the mess away before it could stain the grout between the tiny ceramic tiles.

House-pride is implied by the quick cleaning of the spill. Or is it?

When the shower stopped running, I turned off the radio. Mike liked jazz, so I only listened to two songs before he came out.

This is an unconscious admission—the character is revealing more than she realizes. She is trying too hard to please her husband at the expense of her own desires.

At least they were good ones. "Dreams" by Fleetwood Mac and "Running on Empty" by stone fox Jackson Brown.

Mike looked a little like Jackson Brown. He had the same full lips and the straight shiny hair. He kissed me at the front door. He was carrying a briefcase, not a guitar, which was fine with me. I'd dated more loser musicians than I liked to remember.

First hint at why she might be so willing to please him at her own expense.

"Pork chops," Mike said, a normal happy husband giving his wife instructions for dinner.

And this is where his character becomes clear. He's the man of the traditional household; it's understood between them that he makes the rules and she obeys them.

Without ever telling readers that my decision to pursue poetry was my first major act of rebellion in a gender-biased marriage, the idea becomes clear.

Exercise 10: Align Character to Setting

Character and setting are so closely linked that one continually informs the other in subtle ways. Locate your characters in their natural setting. Where are they? At work? In a house? Which room? Describing setting lets the reader make concrete visual connections; they're not just reading about a character floating in space. Also, choose significant objects to place in the setting, things that link emotionally to the character. Doing this will evoke emotion in the reader, too. And that's always a good thing.

Describe more of the setting you've placed your character in. What is this character's age? If of working age, what kind of job does she have? Does she like or dislike it? Where does she live? How much time does she spend in the room where the current action is taking place? What are the things in the room that are important to her? Is she sitting or standing?

If you're writing memoir, chose a time in your life you particularly want to revisit. You'll be amazed at the details you remember. I still remember my phone number and address from age five, the pink bedspread on my twin bed, and the ballerina lamp on my dresser.

A Note on She

At the time I'm writing this, there is no non-gender specific singular pronoun. "They" is becoming more common, but sticklers still frown upon it, because it's historically plural. "He or she" is politically correct, but cumbersome. "S/he" is my own invention, and I rather like it, but my editors find it annoying. My answer to this dilemma is for women writers to use "she" and male writers to use "he." I wish the rest of the world would heed my obvious solution. Meanwhile, men, don't be offended. Of course I mean "he or she" every time I write "she."

Character and Gesture

Character is action. What are the things she does that reveal who she is? Does she have a nervous tick or a signature gesture she uses when under stress? How does she feel about her body? Action speaks louder than words. Your goal is to write scenes that show rather than tell your character's story.

Example: In my story, I'm barefoot. (Shows I'm casual) Oblivious to lurking germs, (Shows I'm no science major) I have to be told (Shows I'm a bit childlike) to put on my shoes. My husband is willing to take on the parental role, maybe a bit too willing. (Shows his desire for control) But when, at the end of the day, I'm too tired to cook dinner, I am able to stand up for myself. (Shows I'm not totally passive) Although my husband refuses to go out to dinner (Shows he's still the boss), he agrees to having pizza delivered. (Shows he's willing to compromise.)

Exercise 11: Write a Scene

Write a scene that shows the dynamic between two people who basically want the same thing (In my case, a happy marriage—but you can use anything, even the last Coke in the fridge.) but block each other from achieving it. Resist every urge to tell what they want or how they feel. Instead, use setting and gesture to show.

Conflict

You want a story not just about any average day in the life of your character, but the day that is different, the day everything changes for them. In a coming of age story, that's the day they take a giant step into becoming an adult.

On this day, something or someone is threatening your character's status quo, worsening the trouble, forcing the character to react, initiating conflict. Conflict, and how the character handles it, is the core of story.

Antagonist

Popular stories use people to illustrate conflict. Not just to depict good versus evil, but even more subtle than that, the way each of us is in some way in relentless pursuit of our own most burning desire, and how other people get in our way.

Often, protagonist and antagonist have something in common. They both want the same thing, like a happy marriage. But they may define this differently, or have conflicting although equally compelling motivations.

The bad guy is just as important as the good guy. And the bad guy is not necessarily evil. Antagonists are only bad in that they threaten the peace and happiness of protagonists. Therefore, put together an antagonist as carefully as your protagonist. Give him/her something of yours, something you love. This will give you insight into the "bad guy." Make this character fully dimensional, not a stereotypical flat antagonist. My ex-husband was not a bad person. He loved me. He was good to me. But he also grew up in a household with distinct gender roles. And I don't think he'd ever met a poet in his life.

Creating a fully developed antagonist will make the struggle between your characters more compelling.

In literary and experimental stories, antagonists can be groups (think the KKK to a black southern man in 1950s). Man vs. evil, man vs. nature, man vs. self. These are more internal conflicts, which are more difficult to articulate, particularly on film, so if you're interested in publishing commercial stories, sticking to a flesh and blood individuals as antagonists will help sell your work. If you wish to write for a more literary or edgy audience, the market narrows but the choices widen.

Relationships

It's interesting if the protagonist and antagonist have the same flaw. If they both start out at the same level in the story, the protagonist grows and changes, but the antagonist does not. Or in my case, both change and grow, just in opposite directions.

Also, if the protagonist's own actions and personality has brought on the trouble, as with my inability to clearly see that I was not a typical 1950s housewife like my mother, but a 1970s poet, that makes the internal conflict and external growth even clearer.

Think about ways your characters can play off each other's strengths and weaknesses.

Exercise 12: Strengths & Weaknesses

Using the protagonist/antagonist scene from Exercise 11 as a starting point, list each character's top five strengths and then their weaknesses. Use these in your story, if appropriate.

Your Story

If you haven't begun to already, start a story, real or imagined. Use the writing exercises or your notebook to prompt you, or not. It's up to you. The basic map is Beginning, Middle, End, but you don't have to write it in that order. Nor do you have to keep in mind any of the story elements I've been talking about. Let them come to you naturally, if they want to. Otherwise, don't worry, just do your thing.

This is a first draft, so write exactly what your heart dictates. There will possibly be a voice whispering into your ear, telling you your story is crap, a mess, completely stupid. Ignore this voice. Who cares if your story is crap, a mess, or completely stupid? Nobody's going to see it but you. You'll fix it later. I'll show you how.

If you're the type who likes a more detailed roadmap, here are some suggestions. For now, they're just suggestions. Don't worry if your story doesn't follow the pattern. It doesn't have to.

1. Beginning:

A strong main character with a clear goal in a setting appropriate to theme. Theme is simply the meaning behind the story: why the character desires this goal. My theme might be something like "Marriage cannot survive if wife's desire is overruled by husband."

2. Middle:

An equally strong opposing character thwarts this goal. Both characters should have solid motivation for why they want this goal. Tension in story should increase as protagonist goes after goal and antagonist blocks. The increasing beats of tension in my story might be listed as coffee spill, music off, pork chops, poems, flood, feet, poems again, pizza.

3. Conclusion:

Crisis/climax brings story to an effective end. The climax of my story is when I decide to save my poems (and not cook dinner) at the risk of annoying my husband.

Optional Epiphany:

An epiphany, the last sentence or paragraph in some stories, is an insight or sudden revelation by the main character serves to taper off the story so reader understands a change has occurred. Not all contemporary writers use epiphanies. My epiphany was in realizing that my writing life had not finished when I became a wife. I learned that I could deliberately decide to write, without waiting for inspiration or permission.

After the Story: Adding Layers

Using the right details adds layers of complexity to a story. Details are one of the ways a creative writer shows instead of tells. The right details give subtle hints about what the writer wants to convey to the reader. Some details are concrete. Some are symbolic. The best are both. A shiny coffee pot perking on a kitchen counter is a coffee pot, but it's also a symbol of domestic life. And the fact that it's shiny, not smudged, indicates that the person who owns it is proud of her things, and takes care with them.

Props set the story stage; they are integral to the setting and so must have significance. Props can express character or theme, or, best of all, both.

Take the basement clothesline in "Death of the Only Living Poet." The story character at first hangs wet rags on the clothesline as she finishes wiping up after a flood. Later, instead of throwing them away, she hangs her wet poems up to dry, clipping them to the line with clothespins. This echoes her earlier action, but also sends a subtle signal: this character no longer puts housework above creative work. And the whole idea of location is there on a subconscious level, too. In purely symbolic language, a house is often equated with a human body, and a basement stands for the subconscious, the things below our conscious level of thought. My artist self has gone underground (in the basement, boxed up) as I adjusted to married life. Then the flood forces me to choose between throwing away my poems, the expressions of my creative self, or reawakening that part of my personality. When I furnish a room on the main floor of my home with typewriter and table, I honor my writing self and integrate that part of me into full consciousness.

One of the traits of a successful character in a story is that they must have the opportunity to grow, to change. When a character goes through a process of mental restructuring, we call this their arc. In most fiction, arcs move from less positive to more positive. In coming of age stories, a character matures, acquires a piece of new knowledge and is better able to handle life in the adult world.

One way to illuminate character arc is by observing how they react to increasing pressure, either internal or external. Grace under pressure, keeping your cool, figuring out solutions to problems, facing difficult choices, fighting fears—these are all ways to show character growth.

A subtle way to show character growth is to use the details in your story to contrast early and later behavior. Movement of creative energy from basement to main floor. **FROM** doing everything a partner has come to expect, like clipping wet laundry to a clothesline **TO** taking a stand for the personal need for a creative outlet, like clipping wet poems to the same clothesline.

Extending a metaphor, that is, bringing an object like my clothesline back for two or more scenes, is tricky to do well in a short story. You don't want the reader to feel like they're being hit over the head with the hammer. Readers know stuff without everything having to be spelled out, even if they don't consciously think about it, they get it at least on a subliminal level.

An example of going overboard with an extended metaphor would be if the wife in my story used that clothesline to tie her husband to a chair while forcing him to read her poems. That's overkill.

It's a delicate balance, but don't be afraid to use extended metaphors. Your story will be richer for it.

Exercise 13: From Detail to Metaphor

Look at your story. What are the details? List five details, concrete items, things you can touch, see, and feel, that you've included in your story. Why are these details there? Do they serve a purpose beyond the obvious? A pair of glasses on a face means someone needs vision correction. But does this character also have another, less obvious attribute? Maybe they can't spot trouble standing right in front of them.

For each detail you've listed, try to go deeper into why you chose it. Much of writing is done on a subconscious level—the story seems to write itself. You might not know why you put the gun on the seat of the car. Your pen just put it there. That's your subconscious, your story mind.

Taking note of the details in your story will allow you to deliberately manipulate and expand them, so that the reader will feel a more subliminal kick. Enriching your details through metaphor gives your story power.

Exercise 14: Extending Metaphor

Is there a place in your story where you've used a concrete detail two ways? Does it signify a mental shift in your character? If not, can you think of something that would?

FOUR

Short Story

"Literature is not an instruction manual."

Charles Baxter

Breaking the Rules

Before I knew the rules of story, I just wrote them. After all, I'd been a high school outsider. I'd once been all about breaking rules. Now I was a married woman who loved reading short stories when not baking perfect pork chops or buffing her stainless steel coffee pot to a high shine. Writing them seemed the next natural thing.

In 1967, Joyce Carol Oates wrote "Where Are You Going, Where Have You Been?" Some years later, I read it, and still remember the impact of the final lines. The book open on my lap as I stared out my window at nothing. Part of me was baffled. What did it mean? Why didn't Oates say what happened when Arnold Friend took Connie for that final ride?

Another part of me was overtaken by a kind of bliss, enraptured with words, determined to become smart enough to figure out what those kinds of stories, the edgy ones without an epiphany tacked to the end to sum up what the character learned, were saying.

I was ready to move on from poetry. I still loved reading slim volumes by Pablo Neruda, Rilke, Elizabeth Bishop, Charles Wright, and Sylvia Plath. I pored over the Emily Dickinson's *Final Harvest* and Walt Whitman's *Leaves of Grass.* Reading poetry became a life-long pleasure. It keeps me close to what made me fall in love with words in the first place.

Reading poetry was both my pleasure and my problem. After penning hundreds of my own poems, I couldn't help but compare myself to the masters. And, even though lots of little magazines printed my poems, I knew I was not even close to their level. I realize now, that if I'd kept at it, I would have improved. Writing gets better with practice. But I didn't know that then, I thought I'd practiced enough, thought I'd do better with stories.

After dozens of terrible tries, finally something good. A magazine published "Musical Notes & Lofty Theories" and even sent me a check. All I'd received for my published poems, and this is still standard, were contributors' copies: an issue or two of the journal in which my work appeared. Here's an epiphany: stories were much more lucrative.

Exercise 15: Epiphany

You should be well into the second or third draft of your own story now. Will your character experience an epiphany? If so, what will it be? Write a paragraph explaining the character's growth or lack of growth throughout the story. Why did you make this choice?

Breaking More Rules

As you read the following short story, notice that it breaks a lot of rules. There's more summary than scene, and it's short but stretches over long months, shattering Aristotle's unity of time. There's no epiphany.

Another thing about this story that breaks a rule, at least of popular fiction, is that readers don't like characters in the arts. Or so one editor of popular novels told me. My main character, Greta, is a writer and musician. Then, at a writer's conference, a literary editor claimed waitresses were cliché. Greta's antagonist, Daisy, is a waitress.

There are different rules for popular and literary stories, but they shift on a daily basis. More than rules, these editorial whims about what kinds of characters will captivate readers change all the time. What editors, both popular and literary, really want are interesting, compelling characters. The editors of *Room of One's Own* believed I'd done that.

Musical Notes & Lofty Theories

I love my guitar and my typewriter with equal intensity, an intensity that quite diminishes all other earthly choices. So what it comes down to mainly is me always agonizing over dividing myself creatively. I have lots of short-term relationships with men to divert myself from my main dilemma, but they usually end when he starts to absorb too much of my time.

Finally I move into a flat, the upper floor of an old house, because the tenant below is another musician I know vaguely from clubs around town. His name is Max and he is safely married to Daisy.

The first time I meet Daisy, she comes upstairs, hugging this hugely protruding belly, determined to know me. I open my door and see her precariously balanced on my step and I have to let her in. I've been playing my guitar and she glances at it as she plops, with a whoosh, onto my sofa.

"I used to sing in high school," she tells me, "though I never finished. School I mean. I didn't see no sense in it. I was in love with Max already and I knew someday we'd get married and he would take care of me anyhow. That was four years ago. Last month he finally got around to doing it and not a bit too soon as you can see . Are you a musician, too?"

"Um, not really, I guess. It's just sort of fun."

"Well, cuz I seen you going out in the evenings and then gettin' in after bar hours, same as Max, so I figured--"

"I'm a bartender downtown. Sometimes during the day I take classes or write."

"Well, you sure do play good if it's just for fun. Max is real serious about his music; imagine, someday, he wants to be in the Detroit Symphony! Do you know any Fleetwood Mac?"

I play "Say You Love Me" and Daisy sings, and I play "Love in Store" and Daisy sings some more. At last she says her back is hurting and she trundles down the stairs to her and Max's place. I can't watch her descent: gravity working against fate with every step.

In June, Daisy goes to the hospital, then home to her Ma's for a couple of weeks to recover and get help with the baby. I sit on the porch, spring flowers blow in warm wind, wind steals the notes as I play them on my guitar.

Max and I come to be porch friends. We talk about music, which I love in a secret, intense way that I've never really been able to communicate to anyone before Max. From the first, I believe he understands.

We are, Max and I, wary of each other, as people who feel an impossible attraction will be. Daisy is here, of course, sprouting up between us like spring, glowing sweetly and quite unaware of anything that does not immediately concern her baby, who turned out to be a girl named Samantha, who is called Sammy.

Spring saunters into summer, and Daisy eventually goes to work as a cashier at the Lazy-El Steak House. Max works evenings, so the care and feeding of little Sammy naturally falls to him, and almost imperceptibly at first, to me, too. Max is an excellent father and genuinely does not mind, no, in fact he relishes his new role. Sammy always smells so sweet, always has a clean sun suit on, always has a smile on her toothless, smudgeless face.

If Max hears me clomping down the stairs, he calls "Greta, Sammy's eating scrambled eggs for the first time and she loves them!" or "Sammy laughed out loud just now when she heard your clogs on the steps!" Sammy becomes a never-ending source of amusement and wonder. She becomes the possibility on which hundreds of conversations can be struck up. And eventually are.

Winter passes. I get a cat; Daisy becomes quiet and serious. Max takes a job playing cello during cocktail hour. Sammy grows.

Suddenly, Max and I are on the porch again, watching Sammy as she fearlessly ambles forward, first supporting herself by holding onto the rails along the sides of the porch, and then letting go after a bit, clapping her hands and proudly walking right up to Max and giggling in his face. She is so clearly delighted, squealing, "Sam go, Dad, Sam go!"

Later, we're still sitting there; it's one of the first really warm spring days. Max has put Sammy down for a nap and brought out a couple of beers, we're feeling real good between the sun, and Sammy, and it being Monday, our mutual day off. Before we know it, it's 4:30 and Daisy drives up from work, looking none too fresh or even much pleased with the day. Max tries to cheer her with the news of Sammy walking but she bursts into tears and slams into the house, waking the baby, who cries for Max.

I get out of there and into my own place, but I still hear Daisy crying, and Max solemnly playing his cello.

Even though I try to tell myself I love Max only as a dear friend, I'm not sure it's true.

I try to believe it's only string instruments, only the common work hours, the same taste in books, in beer. I tell myself that it's my affection for Sammy that brings me downstairs so often. But secretly I know it's more than anything I can admit to Max. Or to myself.

So how does Daisy know what my heart never even dared to whisper? Because, sitting in my lonely room, listening to her tears blend with the signs of Max's strings and bow, I know I love him. And he loves me. And Daisy knows too. In less than a week, she and Sammy are gone.

From my tiny window upstairs, the window that my desk and typewriter are under, the window where I watch the world and report it, I see Daisy and Sammy leave. It's early, before noon, anyway. I know Max is still asleep. They just get into a cab and go and all day I imagine them at the train station, Daisy glancing around, surprised at her adventure. I see her clutching Sammy and stepping onto a train.

I don't feel good that they've gone, or actually that Sammy's gone. Max definitely loves her more than any other person ever, and I know the loss must kill him. There's no way I want him to feel so bad. I wish I'd moved away first. Left them to their life, deleted them like an awkward paragraph.

As it is, my romance with Max is predictably bittersweet, and if it is love, which I think it is, it certainly hurts more than anything ever. But I try to believe that it only hurts because I know it has to end.

I said Max loves me and he does. But how can he respect our love when it caused him to lose his baby girl? Oh, in the first terrible despair, he clings to me, he makes love to me like he'll never let me go. But as grief subsides and intellect takes over, that voice of reason shouts that lust and like ideals are nothing at all next to the love a parent carries for his child. And Max feels weak for having befriended me, weak because he was sure, from the minute we became porch friends, that he could easily love me much more than Daisy.

I won't go on about our wonderful weeks, our rapturous evenings, because in truth the beginning of our affair is only the beginning of the end of us. I feel it.

On a night in the latest summer, lying with me among the twisted white sheets of my bed, his eyes veiled and looking toward the moon, Max says "Sammy and Daisy are coming home."

I cry. I kiss him. I tell him how happy I am for him. He looks so sad to hurt me that I give him as honest a hug as I can sand say it doesn't matter, Sammy's coming home, only that matters.

I'm packing my books and my guitar, my records and my typewriter, my clothes and my pots and manuscripts; and I'm not worried about love or trying to decide if I should write or play the guitar. I'm not worried about anything, actually. I'm not even really thinking about Max, who is downstairs whistling, probably fixing himself a sandwich.

I am thinking about Daisy, someone so different from me, someone who never had any pretensions toward art to occupy her, who merely believed that because Max was her man he would take care of her. Her assumption was in no way ludicrous; neither were her pain and confusion when she was set smack in the middle of the real world with a baby who could not be fed musical notes and lofty theories. Daisy of the Steak House till, Daisy who worked all day and all night and who was denied that inalienable right of all mothers everywhere to see their daughters' first steps. Daisy with her bravery and her strength and her inner core of pragmatic good will. Daisy is coming home, and she will thrive.

Morality

Inevitably, individual world view colors fiction. Your own moral standards makes your story abut something more than just a person with a dilemma. Ethics, morals, values, religious conviction (or lack thereof), political beliefs--our deepest, truest sense of how the world works is revealed in our fiction, whether we plan it that way or not.

Students in my literature classes often dislike the loose morals of literary characters. I'll always remember fondly the self-righteous student who indignantly claimed, after reading Hemingway's "Hills Like White Elephants" that the author was "Teaching us how to drink!" Rather than showing us how to live, writers shine light on certain human behavior, not necessarily endorsing it.

Greta has an affair with a married man, but she doesn't revel in it and, in the end, she's the one who gets hurt most by her actions.

In the story, I never say "Don't mess with married men." I don't have to. While I make no moral judgments about Greta, her romantic situation is not something readers are likely to want to emulate.

Readers don't want to be preached to, unless their choice of text is the Bible. Even writers of children's literature should be wary of putting too much emphasis on the notion of the way things should be or the way good people should behave. Showing characters in their natural behaviors, flaws and all, and then the consequences of their actions is fine, as this allows the action to speak for itself, allows the reader to be the judge of what is fair or unjust or joyous or sinful.

Money

The check from my first published short story stretched just far enough for me to learn that I could be a story writer, but I'd have to earn rent money another way, so I decided to finish school. I'd already taken a couple of writing classes at the local community college, so I figured I'd complete my degree, find a teaching job, and have summers to write.

In between research papers, exams, and literary essays, I wrote another story. "Cherry Vanilla" won top honors (and another fat check) in a college competition. I say this not to brag, but to point out that although I was now being paid for my writing, it was not nearly enough to support myself. Most writers, I discovered, had day jobs.

Cherry Vanilla

Summer 1967. I am eleven years old, sitting at the dinner table with Mama and Daddy, Danny and Pat, and my three little sisters.

"They're burning up Detroit this time," Daddy said, disgusted.

"What the hell do they want now?" Pat asked.

"Who the hell knows. This whole civil rights bullshit."

"Civil rights means all folks are equal. Sister Mary Margaret says we're all brothers and sisters under God." It just popped out of my mouth. I thought Daddy might be proud of me for knowing so much, but he simply backhanded me, hitting me in the mouth, knocking me from my chair to the floor, where I sat, lips stinging, too stunned to cry.

My little sisters all put their eyes to their plates. So did Mama.

"Go to your room, Miss, and think about this. If you ever marry one of them, you're no daughter of mine."

I went to my room and I thought. I thought I would like to die, but it was a sin against Jesus. I thought I would like to run away, but where would I go? I thought, will I really marry some day?

Then I basically forgot about racism until I came to be around more black folks on a daily basis that I had ever seen in my life. It happened when I enrolled in night classes at City College. City was a black school and I was fresh out of St. Anne's, still living in my unofficially segregated Irish neighborhood with Mama.

I helped her with the girls. Daddy had met up with a barmaid he couldn't say no to and left Mama and all of us kids without a backward glance. I guess the boys went over to see him once in awhile. They were all in the house-painting trade and saw each other at union meetings, too. I never saw Daddy, and I missed him. He was a sweet guy when he was sober.

My little sisters used to ask me, their little voices full of heartbreak, if Daddy would ever visit. After awhile, they stopped asking. I'd tried to get Mama to arrange something, but she'd gotten so upset when I brought up the subject that she started beating her chest and out came the rosary. We said a special novena after she told me through tears that a daughter must never forsake her mother for a whore.

Poor Mama. She could never get any child support out of Daddy and had to go on welfare. The social worker told Mama about this tuition payment program for vocational education, such as clerical work. The social worker said she could fix it so I could go to business school and become an asset to the family.

During the course of my training I had to take a few regular classes like Business English and Algebra. For these, I attended City. When I got my certificate, instead of being proud or happy, I was sad. I wanted to stay at City and finish a real degree. Without telling Mama, I applied for a scholarship, and was accepted.

"I was praying for the day you'd be bringing home a paycheck," Mama said.

"But, Ma," I reasoned as I plaited my little sister's hair, "I can make about double a secretarial salary if I get, say a job as a social worker, like Ms. Adams." Ms. Adams was our caseworker.

"You get your intelligence from my side of the family," Mama said, which is when I knew it would be okay. I could stay in school.

George Andrews was my Natural Science lab partner. Our first project was to dissect a rat. George picked him up by the tail and split open his hairy white belly with a sharp blade. We found that he was a her when our dissection revealed a tiny sack of dead rat embryos. They were almost full term. George got almost as white as me, said something under his breath, and left the room.

He didn't come back to class at all that day. I was left to dig out the intestines and kidneys and liver alone. The teacher instructed me to puncture the amniotic sac full of babies and lay them out for the class to observe. They were curled and mysterious, like the pictures of human fetuses I had seen.

After class, George was waiting for me, leaning up against the door. "Shawn, I'm sorry about that back there, but I just got sick when I saw those rat babies," he said, falling into an easy step beside me.

"It's okay, I left the lab report for you to write up," I said, winking as I handed it to him.

"Oh," he laughed at my wink. I think we were both startled. I am not a flirty type girl. "No problem," he said, flushed under his dark skin. "Thanks again, Shawn," he said, turning down a side hallway. I walked along the main corridor in a daze. People of all shades of color, none as pale as I, streamed around me, talking and shouting to each other, saying hello, asking about lunch or the test that afternoon. Nobody spoke to me.

I saw people I knew from class, but even if they were friendly during English or History, they avoided my eyes in the hallway or the lunchroom or at the pub downstairs. Nobody wanted to be seen making nice with the white girl.

My red hair had gotten me teased some at school, but this was different. Two girls looked at each other as I walked into my afternoon class, one of them commenting "Here comes Ms. Peckerwood." Everyone in the cluster at the door giggled. I had no idea what they meant, but I knew it couldn't be good.

Then in history class, the same girl got upset when we were studying the complex race relations during slavery days. "White people is stupid," she said. "They think we less than them but our women raised they babies."

I noticed her use of the singular instead of the proper plural, but didn't say anything, and neither did the teacher, who let her rant and then went on with the lesson. I was still reeling from the slides he'd shown of naked men, women, and children wearing only iron collars and heavy chains while standing on a platform at the slave market, waiting to be sold to the highest bidder. I could feel hostility all around me. It was worse than the time in English class when I ventured a guess that the "white witch" in the poem was cocaine. Then, everyone had laughed at my innocence. Now, it felt like I was branded as guilty.

After class, one guy came up to me and said, "We aren't all like that," and gave my arm a squeeze before he walked off. Another woman, almost as quiet as I was, with sharp high cheekbones and silky hair that didn't quite match her brown skin, came up behind him and asked me if I wanted to go for coffee. I couldn't speak because I was afraid I'd cry, so I just nodded.

"Sometimes I hate black folk," she said, putting a heavy dose of cream into her coffee. "I'm half Native American, but I don't like Indians much, either." She grinned. "I'm Glenda, by the way."

"Shawn."

"I know."

"I can see why people get upset. That slave market was evil."

She waved her hand in the air. "That's in the past. You don't look like you keep slaves." She was staring at my dish soap roughened hands and ragged cuticles. I felt like she could see down to the hole in the sole of my left shoe.

I hoped she would never know about my own racist family.

Dad and the boys were the worst, but even Mama was intolerant. She'd shake her head and sigh when she saw young girls with a baby or two in the welfare office. "They don't care to work," she'd say with a sniff, never for a moment connecting her own situation to theirs.

After awhile, I stopped noticing skin color or speech differences. I became more like myself, which is not to say comfortable or relaxed or confident, but at least friendly and more open. I saw that there were all different kinds of kids, the obviously well off ones with nice clothes and cars and talk of where they went in Europe on vacation, the ones with day jobs that paid okay and allowed them time off for a class or two (George fit into this category), and then the poor people, like me, who you could tell had childhoods marred by drink or drugs or abuse or all of it together. We knew each other instinctively, or maybe just because we saw each other all the time in the financial aid office, where we filled out endless Pell Grant forms.

Glenda and I had coffee almost every day. She was poor like me, but lived alone in a cute little apartment off campus. It was part of a house, upstairs. She took me there once and offered a joint she took from a matchbox.

"I don't smoke," I said.

She narrowed her eyes and giggled. "Ancient ritual, the peace pipe," she said. It wasn't a pipe, and I didn't feel all that peaceful until she shrugged and put the pot away.

She showed me her paintings, all nudes, all of women, all in hues of orange and yellow with brash black slashes for eyes. They were a weird mix of sensual and angry. Later, we went to a club. I was the only white person there. All her friends were nice to me, but they got a little disgusted when I could not pick up the moves to the dances they were doing. It was true, I couldn't tell my left foot from my right. After several drinks, everyone at the table (except me, I drank white wine and soda, since Mama could smell liquor a mile away and would beat me raw if I came home drunk) began to slur their words, even Glenda. I told her I had an early class, and took a cab home.

"Don't feel bad," she said, "just cause you got no rhythm."

“I’ll try not to,” I said, waving at her friends on my way out the door.

I did have an early class, English, my favorite. Then there was Science, which I despised. If not for George, I would never have gotten through. He and I became friends, too. I found out he was an orphan. He had been working his way through college and was determined to make a decent life for himself. I admired that. I respected him so much. He never smoked or drank, he never swore, or got upset. He was even and steady and I wanted his serenity. I was all sharp edges and moods and I was about sick of myself.

George didn’t always have a lot of time between classes. He had a job, and he was the biggest sports fan I’d ever known. If he wasn’t going to work, he was rushing off to watch some football event. He talked with such enthusiasm for the game. But I didn’t care for sports, so football was one of the few things George and I never shared.

We found another common interest, however. I used to hide out in the stacks when I was feeling blue. Nobody ever seemed to come up to the 4th floor where all the psych books were, where I looked day and again for some sample, some case history, of a person like me who was so different from her family, from the people in her neighborhood. I wanted to know I wasn’t the only one and I wanted to know why I was different, what it meant.

One day as I climbed down from my sanctuary, I saw George in the literature section, sitting on the floor in front of the shelves, surrounded by books, reading one with rapt attention.

"Hi." I walked toward him and stood there looking down at him, a big smile on my face. It made me feel good just to look at him. He looked up, his eyes misted with literature, and held out his hand to me. I took it and he pulled me down next to him. "Let me introduce you to my friend Bill Shakespeare," he said.

From then on, we had a love of the past, and poetry, in common. George turned me on to poets who had been dead for a hundred years or more, whose words he had to translate from the arcane for me. My favorite was Neruda. He lived on a little island, Isle Nigra, in a house by the sea that was filled with books. The first gift George ever gave me was a copy of Neruda's book *Twenty Love Poems and a Song of Despair*.

He presented the book to me when I came back to his room. We pretended we'd gone there to study, but at least one of us knew there was more to it. I hoped he'd kiss me. Hell, I wished we'd make love. My physical attraction grew right along with the emotional attachment.

It had started when he'd pulled me to the floor in the library and I'd flashed on us lying surrounded by open books in some eternal kiss. I had that flash and I was embarrassed. Embarrassed and relieved that he could not read my mind.

Then in class I started to notice every time his hand brushed mine, say passing the microscope we shared. Or if our heads bent close together over a problem and I could feel his breath mingling with mine, I would become liquidly electric.

This was new. I had never been in love. Sex, sure, I'd had it. Couldn't see the big deal boys especially made over it. That was all they wanted when they asked me out on dates. The minute they got me alone, the pawing would start. Sometimes, I pretended to enjoy it.

But it had never felt like this, like our natural letting go of books and clothes and lying down beside each other on his single bed. My teenage sweethearts had never head of Keats or Byron or Neruda, they never whispered to me as they kissed every inch of me before moving slowly inside, "Body of a woman, white hills, white thighs, you look like a world, lying in surrender." George quoted Neruda, but it felt like our own secret language.

Later he quoted the same lines in Spanish. The translation he gave me had the original on one side of the page, the translation on the other. So George gave me poetry, in many languages. From that night, our bodies were twined, the black skin and the white, as appropriate and inevitable as a starched shirt inside a tuxedo.

I could never explain to my family. Some kids at school scorned George for mixing with me. The really pretty girls, the ones who would not have given George, or me for that matter, a second glance before we got together, they looked at me like I was poison. They'd ask George why he didn't stick to his own kind. The thing was, George WAS my kind.

Glenda called me a nasty name, but she laughed when she said it, and she sat down with me and George with her coffee cup.

"I am in love," I said, stirring my coffee, "so have a care."

George graduated before I did and was already established with his own company by the time I received my MSW. He told me about a clinic in his building. The staff psychologist was an acquaintance of his and he got me an interview, so we ended up working at the same place. Convenient if not exactly comfortable. Word got around about us, but after time passed, I was immune to sneers and stares. Anyway, city folks are pretty blasé about mixed couples. You see it all the time.

"I have this friend," George said one day at lunch. "She called the receptionist in my office Cherry Vanilla. I guess you can add that to your list of slurs black people have for whites."

I thought it was cute and said so.

"Well, I don't like it," George said. "It's dehumanizing."

His tone was so fierce. It made me wonder about this friend. I hadn't missed the "she" part of the story.

"Does this friend know about us?"

"Yes, she's cool." He wiped his mouth with his napkin and pulled out his wallet to pay the check. The conversation was over. It was time to get back to work.

I didn't forget about his friend, though. She felt like a threat, but I didn't know why. Because she was black? Because they wouldn't think twice about introducing each other to family? Well, George didn't have a family, which made it even more important that he get to share his partner's folks. And I hadn't done one thing about that. I couldn't. My family would freak. George and I were both orphans in a way. Except I still had a family to go home to, and he was not welcome there, had never been invited.

It was time to tell my family the truth, even if it meant the end of my relationship with them. So I was thankful for George's mysterious friend; a woman I didn't even know had helped put something into perspective that have been haunting me since 1967.

I told George my decision and he seemed elated. We made plans to move in together, to really make a life with each other. A few days later, he told me that he was in love with the friend who had likened white redheads to ice cream flavors. He wanted to marry her, he said.

We both cried. He with relief, me because I was losing my best friend and the only man who had ever offered me love, tenderness, and compassion. I'd taken him for granted for so long. I had nobody to blame but myself.

I saw her once, George's new woman. We met on the staircase of my office building. I guess he was on her way to see George. She looked at me as if she knew who I was. Her eyes sort of crumbled before she turned them away. She was so beautiful, and, like the scorned lover in Neruda's *Song of Despair*, I was the abandoned one.

Exercise 16: Impersonal Antagonists

The antagonist in *Cherry Vanilla* is not a person, but thing: racism. Still, many of the characters in the story have unexamined prejudices that reinforce Shawn's struggle against racism. Is the antagonist in your story a person or a thing? If your antagonist is a person, what basic value of your main character do they oppose? Why? How can you show this opposition in a scene? If your antagonist is a thing, imagine a character you might add to the story that will mirror and strengthen the antagonist

Exercise 17: Accomplishments

Quickly list 20 accomplishments in your life, things you're proud of. Look at your list. What does it say about your values? What do you respect in yourself and others? What are your strengths? What weaknesses do you want to improve?

Exercise 18: Values

Write about a difficult ethical, moral, or spiritual decision you (or someone you know, or a character you create) had to make. How did it feel? Don't just name the emotion, think about the physical sensations that accompanied the feelings.

FIVE

Novels

"Start where the trouble starts."

Jennifer Crusie

Chasing Trends

The thing about epiphanies is that in real life, they never turn out to be the big revelation, the sudden truth that changes your life for the better and finally puts you on the right path. I sold a handful of stories over the course of several years, and while the money was nice, it wasn't enough to support me. I'd learned a thing or two about how most fiction writers made their living by this time, and it wasn't entirely by writing, unless they were Stephen King or J. K. Rowling. For steady income, writers taught.

When I learned this, I was a single mom and secretary. I was so poor, I qualified for a Pell Grant. So at the ripe old age of 28, I went back to school, figuring I'd write novels in the summer. Hardly anyone was publishing books of short stories, and even less people bought them. I was certain that a career as a novelist/teacher was the way to go.

But, what kind of novel to write? I'd tried a contemporary called *At the Bar* when I was pregnant with my first son. It was horrible and only 100 pages. Novels need to be at least triple that.

During the madness of a shattering marriage and two babies, I wrote *Rock and Roll Dreams,* which was a little longer, but equally abysmal. Then I split from my husband and in my secretary days took my boss's advice. He read mysteries. He told me they were the hot new trend, and I should write one. So I did. I blame *Murder in the Key of C* on him.

Next I got my family saga out of the way. *Those Turner Sisters* was an homage to my wonderful grandmother and my crazy family. It was also sort of icky. I read somewhere that aspiring novelists should forget about trends and write what they love, which is how I came to write the historical novel *Satisfactory Society.* It was a sweet Regency, the most untrendy sort of book in the world. They don't even publish them anymore. Mine never got published either. It wasn't very good.

Turns out writing a novel every summer is almost impossible, especially if, like me, you want your novel to be good enough to find a publisher. I just didn't have the time. The family cottage I shared with my young sons and new husband was four hours north, and also our favorite place to be, all those barbecues and boat rides and friends popping in for the weekend at the lake.

When my kids got older, got jobs, went off to college, we sold the cottage. I finally had more time to write. But this time, I decided to be smart and research the market. What I discovered is that more than half of all the novels published each year are romance novels. Other genres, like sci-fi/fantasy and thriller, and also popular, but romance is Queen of Book Contracts. I liked those odds, so I wrote *Attracting Jack,* my first and only romance novel.

And because the romance world is full of lovely people, the editor to whom I sent it actually wrote a personal rejection letter in reply instead of the usual form rejection letter literary agents sent. The romance editor said, as kindly as possible, that I needed to work on my craft.

This puzzling piece of information turned out to be the best advice I've ever received. Here's why I was mystified by her comment. By this time, I had two degrees in English literature. I taught writing at a university. I reviewed fiction for respected magazines. Shouldn't I know craft?

Certainly I knew language. I had word craft. I could write a killer essay. Editors loved my book reviews. Because I loved reading novels, I fell into the book critic thing. I'd taken some time off teaching to finally write a decent novel, so it was nice to make a little money, and to finally be paid again for my writing. I earn less reviewing than those stories paid, but I like the work and I'm good at it.

So, since I read and give my opinions about novels, and teach writing and literature to boot, why did I not have a clue how to sustain a novel of my own?

I'm not blaming the system, but the literature programs where I obtained degrees did not emphasize structure so much as study symbolism and critical theory. Plot is sort of a dirty word in some college classes.

As for reading, I loved literature so much that I immediately dropped into what John Gardner calls the "vivid, continuous dream" of a book, never giving a single thought to how the author constructed her story. I figured it just happened.

Maybe for some people. But, as that kind editor pointed out, I needed help. And so after having written five or six novels, I began to seriously study craft. There's nothing I love more than learning a new skill, and I went at it with energy and passion. I read books, took classes, went to workshops, joined critique groups. And finally wrote a novel an agent agreed was worth selling. I didn't follow any trend, just wrote a book I thought would be fun to read.

Crafting a Long Story

Short stories and personal essays differ from novels and book-length memoirs in more than page counts. Novels and book-length memoirs need bigger stories, subplot layering, turning points, and reversals.

Short stories and personal essays are built scene by scene, and so are novels and memoirs. Every scene, in any of these forms, is a unit of increasing (or sometimes decreasing) conflict: a beginning, a middle, and an end. These units of conflict can be goals blocked, problems solved, twists added, plans gone awry. Two major things keep the readers' interest through a long story. Subplots layer in their own, thematically related, goals, conflicts, and resolutions. Reversals and turning points unexpectedly shake up the plot, moving things in new directions.

The Causal Chain

One way to keep a long story organized is to think of it in units of a causal chain. The events in popular novels are structured in such a way as to keep the reader turning pages, interested in both plot and the character.

Starting with a sympathetic character who has a burning desire is key. Putting that character in a situation that erects believable obstacles to this desire requires a well-thought-out plotline.

First draft, I get a character with a true desire and then just write. I want the plot to come about organically; I want my subconscious creative brain to hand me over some juicy material. That usually happens, but the material always has to be shaped later, during the revision process, into a form that will ensure an elegant yet highly readable structure.

Most popular and some literary novels follow a causal chain. That is, as events unfold, things don't happen to the characters in random, unconnected ways. One action results in consequences that spur another action, resulting in a third action, and so on, until the final scene.

In this way, story plot rises organically from the choices a character makes. This is where the growth and twists come in: don't always have your characters and their actions result in the usual ways. This creates predictable plots that bore readers. Characters should take actions to solve a problem standing in the way of their goal or desire, but instead of working out as expected, the actions have an opposite or unexpected effect, making the goal further out of reach, testing the character's mettle, forcing them to grow and change.

Here's where the real work of writing comes in: cause/effect can be knee-jerk, cliched. Of course if she steals a kiss with an old boyfriend, the new boyfriend will walk into the room. Of course if he goes down into the basement to see what the noise is, an intruder with a hatchet hacks off his head.

To avoid the easy, expected plot development, think hard, do a lot of journaling, come up with long lists of possible ways an event can cause havoc. For some reason, golden ideas are usually buried about six items down the brainstorming list.

You'll know you're on the right track when you can create a causal chain like the one I've done below. First, read the summary of the main plot of my novel,

Remodeling Eden. Then go over the linked chain of cause and effect that clearly documents every turn my story takes.

Remodeling Eden Synopsis

Divorced Eve Delacroix risks everything when she attempts to turn six dilapidated hunting cabins into shabby chic cottages. With a tight budget and two months until tourist season, Eve can't afford mistakes, or even furniture in her living quarters.

Realtor Jane Augustine slyly undermines Eve's ability to complete the project. Jane wants Eve's property for herself, to fulfill an old dream that just won't die. But Eve isn't tempted to sell. She's pretty sure that Adam, the town's smitten bank manager, will come through with a business loan.

Then the loan falls through and Eve learns Jane's father owns the bank. Unwilling to give up her dream and let Jane win, Eve ditches her pride and asks her parents for help. With a new fail-proof plan, and cabins filled with a work crew, Eve moves forward with her project. Then, days before she's due to open, someone covers the newly painted cottages with spray-painted hate messages. Eve suspects Jane is behind the vandalism, but she can't prove it. By this time, Eve is physically exhausted and doesn't see a way how to go on until her friends, old and new, surprise her with a painting party that raises her spirits and erases the graffiti.

One of the old friends is Mark, a man Eve loved when they were both married to other people. Eve isn't proud of that part of her past, and has tried to bury it, but when a newly single Mark comes back into the picture, she thinks maybe fate's giving her a chance to set things right. Despite her burgeoning relationship with Adam, the pull of the past is strong.

Almost immediately, Eve finds out how wrong she's been to trust Mark. She'd been so starved for affection in her marriage that she'd mistaken Mark's idea of a casual fling for the real thing. At 38, she feels like a fool, like she's learned nothing about relationships in all her years on the planet. If she'd been smart, she would never have let Adam go. But pride, and the necessity to concentrate on the numerous final details of her project, stop her from asking Adam for another chance. Or even answering his calls about a repair he'd offered to make on her rotted beach stairs.

The night before Eve's cottages are due to open for business, the neglected beach steps cause the death of a young townsperson, Kira. Kira's mother vows to sue Eve and take everything she owns. For the first time, Jane's purchase offer tempts Eve. With one signature, she can settle things with Kira's mother, distance herself from Adam, and abandon the scary prospect of being her own boss.

Then blood tests reveal that Kira was intoxicated when she fell. While this absolves Eve of legal responsibility, it does little to alleviate her remorse or the town's grief. However, the revelation that her ex-husband has restarted an affair he'd carried on with Jane (and concealed from Eve their entire marriage) and that the two of them have conspired to force her to sell, gives Eve the necessary push to reaffirm her commitment to her new life.

As she makes the decision to see her plans through, Eve struggles to find a way to assist Kira's mother, who has been flattened by her loss. Eve organizes a memorial service to mourn Kira's passing and honor her short life. When three male friends of Kira's show up at the wake, one of them confesses to Eve that Jane hired them to vandalize her property.

As formal charges are prepared against Jane, Eve opens her cottages for business and gets an unexpected second chance with Adam.

The Chain

1. Because she gets a lake property in her divorce, Eve, who wants more than anything to be independent and make her own living as her own boss, decides to become an innkeeper in a town hours from where she has lived all her life.
2. Because the place needs a lot of repair, and she has very little cash until she can open her lake cottages for business, she applies for a loan, and meets Adam, a loan officer at the bank. The loan seems like a sure thing, as Eve's property is worth a ton of money and she owns it free and clear.
3. *Loan is denied. (First reversal—or unexpected event.)
4. Because the loan is denied, independent Eve needs financial help from parents to help get her project finished in time for summer.
5. *Because Jane wants the land for herself, she hires kids to destroy Eve's property just as it's finally suitable for rental. (Second reversal.)
6. Because of the vandalism, less-independent-than-ever Eve now needs to call on friends, old and new, for help reviving the cottages
7. Because she asks for help, Eve is reunited with Mark, an old love, complicating her budding relationship with Adam.

8. Because of Mark, Eve resists contacting Adam about her beach steps, which he had offered to repair.
9. *Because her beach steps are in disrepair, someone falls and dies, and her cottages are closed down by the city the day before the first guests are due to arrive. Meanwhile an investigation into the vandalism takes place. (Final reversal. All is lost. Reader cannot see how things will ever work out, how Eve will ever achieve her goal.)
10. Because Eve gives up her quest to be an independent innkeeper, and instead focuses on making amends for the accidental death on her property, everything is resolved: She gets the proof she needs to nail Jane, the truth about the beach steps accident is revealed, Eve and Adam reunite, and the cottages open for business.

About Reversals

Reversals, also known as turning points, shake the story up. Too few reversals, and the book is predictable. Too many reversals and the reader doesn't have time to process the story. Three somewhat evenly spaced turning points are about right. The last turning point, sometimes referred to as "the black moment" when all seems truly lost, is the most dire. The reader should have no idea how things will resolve, or if they think they know, they should be wrong. Avoid the easy out in all reversals, but make sure there is seemingly no way out in the final one.

Exercise 19: Your Chain

Using the story you already wrote, or the new one you are working on, create a causal chain. Make sure the reversals grow more serious each time (and three is the magic number for reversals in novels, but there might only be one in a short story), with the final reversal serving as one of the blackest moments in the character's life: the thing they desire is forever lost (or so it seems). There should be no hint of a way out of the dilemma; the reader should be totally clueless about how things will resolve.

Exercise 20: Same Story Different

You might wonder why I just gave you the plot of my novel. Won't somebody steal it? No. Or, maybe, but it doesn't matter. Give 25 people the same basic plot and you will get 25 completely different stories. Let's try it. Write a one or two page story, whatever you can do in 20 minutes, about a man who loses his baseball cap, a unique cap that is not readily available. He later unexpectedly meets his wife on the street. She is with a man he does not know. Man #2 is wearing a hat exactly like his. What happens next?

When we read these, you will see how many different ways people will play this out.

Six

Children's Lit

"Home is an ordinary gorgeous sentence

that is doing its work."

Carole Maso

The Collaboration

"Cyn," my mom said into the phone. "I've written something."

Filled with dread, I replied, "That's nice."

"Will you read it?"

There is, of course, only one possible answer to that question. So I said yes, promised to stop by later in the week, and tried not to panic. But a question of my own circled relentlessly: How could I critique my mother?

Days of agonizing contemplation followed. Then I came up with the same solution I'd used my entire life: I'd just lie and say it was fine. Everything was fine. Great, in fact. Super. Having made that momentous decision, I took myself to my mother's house for lunch and a look see.

It felt so weird. My mom, having been busy popping out three kids by the age of 18, never got a chance to finish high school, yet she's always been a reader. By the time I was twelve, she automatically passed her paperback Victoria Holt, Catherine Cookson, and Taylor Caldwell novels on to me.

Mom had been a writer, too. She'd sent some short stories to school with me when I was in third grade. My teacher, Mr. Potter, profusely complimented them and drove me home from school in his convertible. I learned later that he'd tried to date my mother, who was, at the time, separated from my dad.

Another one of my mother's many talents is drawing. She sketched for us all the time when we were little. Her mother was a painter, her father a writer. She got both creative gifts, and passed one along to me.

Back at Mom's place, lunch dispensed with, she handed me a spiral notebook. I opened it to the first page, which was covered in single spaced, lightly penciled script. Every page had a drawing or two, too. I read through the story, immediately caught up in the adventures of their cat Sam. And Mom's drawings were great: simple penciled strokes vibrating emotion.

So I didn't have to lie when I said it was great. The only major problem was that she hadn't finished the last part, but instead summarized it. She didn't know how to do it, she said. Could I help? She asked.

I like being a writer because I do it alone. That's the whole point. The story is mine. I am in charge of every single sentence. Also, at this time in my life, I didn't have enough time to work on my own stories, let alone anybody else's. So I told her to try to fix it herself.

“It's great, Mom. Really.” My tone apparently contained a “but.”

"What?" Mom asked.

"Well, some parts, I don't know, is this really for kids?"

"You mean because he dies."

"Yeah, and the bird-stalking."

She tucked the book into a shelf of paperbacks. "You're probably right," she said.

"But I love it. I really do."

A few weeks later I asked Mom if she'd finished the story.

"No, not yet," she said.

Every couple of years, I'd bring it up. After my parents moved from their house to a condo, she said she'd lost it in the move.

Ten years passed. And then a few days before this Mother's Day, something possessed me. I bought her an illustrated book featuring cats. She thanked me profusely even though these days she prefers thick historical novels to slim volumes about cats. I told her the book reminded me of the story she'd once written and asked if she'd ever found it.

"Yes," she surprised me by saying. "Oh, yes, I have it."

There was a note of deep satisfaction in her tone.

"That's great," I said.

Maybe because so many of my writing students want to write children's stories, the idea occurred to me: I should put Mom's cat tale into *Your Words, Your Story*. Mom agreed, although she reminded me about the unfinished ending.

"No problem," I said. "I'll fix it."

Voice

The voice of the story belongs to Sam, a real cat who adopted my parents long after all us kids had left home, but more than Sam, the voice of the story is my mom's. I recognized it. Her natural rhythms and ways of speaking came through. The character of Sam allowed room for interjections of sly humor as well as the precarious balance of light and darkness that is my mother's worldview.

Maybe because she is my mother, I had no trouble dropping down into her voice to finish the story. I typed it up and sent her a copy straight away. See if you can tell where my mom stopped writing and I started.

Sam

By Marjorie Hines

They named me Sam. I like that name. It brings up mysterious images of private investigators, international spies, war heroes, and even one infamous bartender.

My name before I became Sam was Tux, for pretty obvious reasons.

I have a rich grey coat and two similar white spots on the toes of my hind feet. My friend's daughter once called me a handsome fellow. I liked that because it reminded me of when I was Tux, and how I'd gotten that name.

My first family's daughter had said, "He's so handsome, he looks like he's dressed in a fine grey tuxedo." After that, for my first family, I was Tux.

How I arrived at my new home was really my own doing. I'd gotten caught in an awful Michigan snowstorm, the kind that starts out so gently, just nicely falling flakes that any cat worth his salt would like to chase. I was pretending all sorts of things while I played my games and lost track of all time and place.

Suddenly the flakes were falling too fast even for me to keep up with and before I could get my bearings it was sleet that coated me with ice.

I needed shelter.

I spied a big brown truck that had its door open so I jumped inside to have a look.

It seemed a fine place to curl up for a quick cat nap until the awful storm blew through.

As I drifted off to sleep, I could hear someone calling, "Tux, where are you? Here, kitty kitty." I knew I should answer but I was so warm, snuggled among a stack of nice boxes. I decided to stay put for awhile.

I was napping, nicely dreaming a fine dinner when suddenly the box next to me was moved and a voice said, "Hey, how did you get in here?"

I had never heard the voice before. This signaled danger. Any cat worth his salt knows to run from strangers. A quick scan revealed an open door, and just in time. As the stranger reached his hand out to grab me, I bolted, jumping from the truck and landing in a big pile of snow. After a tumble down a hill, I righted myself and took cover under a convenient bush.

I stayed very still. When I heard the truck pull away, I surveyed the area. Nothing was familiar. I needed to get my bearings and decide what to do. The truck, I realized, must have moved while I was napping. I felt a little worried. With all the snow, how would I find my way home?

I was beginning to get hungry, too, but decided another nap was in my best interest, at least until the snow stopped. I scouted the area for a suitable place and spotted a nice little building down the hill.

I made my cautious way toward it, sinking to my chest in wet with every step. This was serious! I looked neither left nor right, just kept the building in my sight at all times, concentrating with clear intent as I moved slowly forward, down the hill, to the building.

I was quite cold, a blob of wet fur with feet coated in ice.

I finally made it to what I deduced at once was a garden shed. The door was the kind that went up and down, not in and out, and the wind had blown a barrier of snow across the entrance. At first, I could not see a way in, but after careful inspection, saw a crack at ground level. The storm had lifted the door just enough for me to dash into my new shelter.

Quite exhausted from my trek down the hill, I took a quick look around.

Good! No strangers. Let's see where I can hide and get warm.

While my mind was occupied with these thoughts, I forgot about being hungry. Then some burlap bags piled into a wheelbarrow invited me to curl up, so I jumped in and settled down.

I awoke suddenly, somehow knowing without a shadow of a doubt that I was in big trouble. I felt kind of sick, and I was really hungry. I crept to the door and peeked out. The night was black; a bare slice of moon lit the crust of ice that had formed over every inch of snow. Tall drifts, some so high I couldn't see over them, glittered.

Everything was still and quiet. Despite the dark and cold, no strangers lurked. I decided to case the joint. Night, after all, is my favorite time.

As I ventured out into the crisp air, exhilaration quickened my breath. I crunched into the ice with each step, my feet going through the thin layer of ice into the snow beneath.

I paused at the shed, rubbing my body against the rough wood and lifting my tail to spray my scent where appropriate, thus ensuring a speedy return to my cozy hideaway, should it become necessary.

Then I was ready for a look see. The snow had stopped; my vision was clear. I crouched as low as I could and sniffed the air. Nothing familiar here. Once again, I felt a twinge of fear. Where was I?

The first thing I needed to do was conduct a thorough investigation of these new surroundings. I noted lots of trees and low shrubbery, and then, up the slope of the hill I had tumbled down earlier, to the side of my shed, a large house. I looked at the house for a long moment, pausing long enough to take in every dark window before I turned my head to see what else was around.

Ice. lots of ice. Reaching clear across, for miles it seemed, before another stand of trees broke its smooth surface. Could this be a lake? Whatever it was, it required closer investigation. I turned from the house toward the large patch of frozen water.

Making my way down to the lake was more difficult than anticipated. It seemed I had not tumbled all the way down the hill. Again I suffered the irritant of thin breaking ice with every step. Finally, at the edge of this mass of ice, which to my satisfaction was indeed a lake, I briefly sniffed something familiar.

I stepped with caution onto the frozen water, lifting one foot off the surface and listening closely for any sound. Not detecting the slightest noise, I knew the ice was solid. I ventured further out, hoping to once again catch that tantalizing scent. Sniffing in all directions, once, then twice, then again. My heart sank as I admitted that there was nothing I knew here. Not one thing.

I was lost. I would never again see the only family I had ever known in the whole five years of my life.

The cold settled over me like a shroud. Sadness and fear took hold. I wanted to be with my family. I wanted my bed, my food dish full of tuna fish, my saucer of water. My hunger came out of my mouth then as a cry, a plea. Maybe they would hear me. Surely they would come for me.

The sound echoed in the cold dark night, but no one answered. No one called my name. What was I going to do? Tough questions are more easily answered with a nap, so I returned to my shed with the burlap bed.

Hunger woke me. *Time to eat*, I thought, not remembering what had happened for the first seconds after I'd awakened. I was not dreaming: I was cold and hungry and lost!

Ah, well. First things first. A good stretch makes everything seem a little less daunting. A cautious trip outside showed trees and shrubs covered with veils of snow and dawn breaking over the roof of the big house on the hill.

Inside the house, a man stood looking out the window. I crouched low; best to stay out of sight. I trained my vision onto his face. His eyes were not looking in my direction. Good. He hadn't spotted me.

Then the most wonderful sight any cat can ever see caught my eye: a bird! The bird ate seeds from a nice, large feeder, close to the man's window. All the shrubs around the ground would be excellent cover, I knew, for the delicious mice who would surely gather to forage for seed husks. Everyone needs to eat. Including me.

Being a house cat, I had never had to hunt for food to survive. Still, it had always been a fond hobby. I was good at it. I make no apologies. Felines are natural predators; I am only following my nature. The wait, the anticipation of the strike, was even more pleasurable for me than the kill.

Usually, the thrill was in the hunt. Today, the hunt meant survival. Gradually, a feeling both ancient and feral came over me. I let it come. It was my birthright.

More birds had joined the first for breakfast, and I felt myself grow large. Large and hungry, no longer a pampered house cat playing games, often letting the birds fly free after I'd caught them. I was now at one with the wild. And soon, at least one of those birds would be one with me.

Every sense alert, I stalked my prey.

Stilling my mind to utter silence, I sharpening every sense and leapt over the earth toward my finely honed bright target, then pounced, teeth bared to grip a red fluttering wing. It fluttered once, twice, and then, no more. I feasted upon the bird.

My great hunger finally satisfied, I took off at a brisk trot toward my shed to have my wash and a nap. Rested, I scouted the hill I'd tumbled down last night, traveling more easily than before, as the bright sun had melted a path, and still melted more, shining down on the diamond cut snow that remained.

I arrived at the street where I'd made my escape from the truck. Surveying all surroundings from this vantage point without the hindrance of icy sleet, I saw before me a busy street I'd do well to keep at a distance. Behind me was the still frozen lake, with barely perceptible eddies swirling underneath the thick ice. To the east was the man's house and west was my own, temporary, I hoped, domain.

I formulated a plan, resolving to come here twice each day, morning and evening, and sit for a time, in the hope that my family would come looking for me. My dearest hope was that they would find me here, waiting. I let out a plaintive cry; a few of these voiced at each sitting would also be a good thing, I thought, in case anyone came searching for me. Another advantage of this daily ritual would be that I could see my new surroundings from this high point on the hillside.

And so began a new life for me, filled with adventures both thrilling and frightening, from each, wonderful or terrible, lessons gleaned.

My first day on the hill was also the second time that I saw the man, the one whom I had seen at the window at dawn. He came out of the garage, which was part of the house, and walked to the road to retrieve his newspaper.

Not quite ready for human contact yet, I stayed low. I was lonely but wary, and wanted to know a few specifics before I gave my trust to a human again. For example, how many people lived with the man? My lost family had two adults and three children.

The oldest child was called Cindy, and she'd been my favorite. She named me, but was also kind to me and respected my wishes when I did not want to be petted or fussed over. Her little brothers paid me no mind, as they favored Duke, a big bothersome dog. The adults didn't pay much attention to me, either, except to take me on torturous trips to the vet office. Except for those yearly shots and the indignity of having my teeth and claws inspected by a stranger in a white coat, the family suited me fine.

Felines don't care for fussing. Our needs are simple: a clean bed, a kind word now and then, freedom to roam, sunshine to rest in, plenty of food and water, a minimum of canine interference, a few strokes under the chin or a cozy lap upon occasion. That is all.

One day melted into the next. I did not change my routine, but I did learn the ways of the big house. The man woke early, near dawn. He walked outside for his newspaper each morning. A woman came to the bird feeder with seed every day.

In the evening, many mice would gather to finish the seed that the birds had scattered on the ground. I became a lion and hunted for food, which was exciting, but not quite enough to make me forget my dish with soft delicious flaked tuna. And I missed the delectable treats that came in crisp foil packages that the girl, I had almost forgotten her name by now, saved for special times.

I had used to receive milk, even cream on occasion, too. Not anymore. It was mice or bird and lake water for me, with a bug here or there for variety. I missed my family. I even missed the dog. But mostly, I missed fine dining.

I sensed it was time to let this family know I was here. I'd start with the man. I saw him every morning from my spot on the hill as he walked to the road for his newspaper. I was always careful to crouch low so he didn't see me. That decisive day, I vowed to let him see me. I was a handsome fellow, after all.

I walked boldly up to him as he came back toward the house with his newspaper.

"Hi, boy," the man said.

I said hi back to him in my own way and did a little dance with him where I wove myself in and out of his feet. He reached down and scratched the top of my head. It felt wonderful. I purred. It had been so long since I'd purred that I startled myself and swiftly ran down the hill toward my shed, away from the man.

The weather was getting warmer, and sometimes the man and woman would sit on the back porch by the bird feeder and look at the lake. I could hear them talking from around the corner, where I remained unseen.

"Have you seen a big cat around here?" the man asked the woman that afternoon.

"No, but if it's the same one who's been killing the birds, we ought to call the pound."

"Now, Marge," the man said, "you love cats."

"Loved. Past tense. It hurt too bad when Toot died. So don't go getting any ideas."

"But if he's killing birds, he must be hungry."

Marge didn't reply.

**

"Hi, boy," the man said, waking me up from a sound sleep in my wheelbarrow. "So this is where you've been hiding."

He came and scratched me on the top of my head again, right between my ears. I arched my neck and he laughed at me and scratched there too.

"Okay, well, I have to cut the grass now. Hope the lawnmower noise doesn't cut into your rest," he said. It would, but that was okay. It was snack time, and I'd spotted a beetle next to the gas can just before I'd closed my eyes.

The man left. Later, he was out on the porch with the woman again.

"You have to admit, he's a darn good mouser," the man said.

"Yes, okay, I'll feed him. But outside. He can't come in." The woman went into the house and came out with a saucer of tuna. I'd know that aroma anywhere. She set it down on the cement, a little too close to the pair of them for my comfort.

"Here, boy, here Sam," the man said. I knew he was speaking to me, because he always called me boy. So Sam was my new name. I'd long ago forgotten the old one. The tuna was too strong a lure to resist, so I trotted out and gobbled it down, right in front of them.

The woman got up and took the saucer from under my nose. "I'll bring him a bowl of milk," she said, barely looking at me.

I turned my face to the man. He was smiling at me and tapping on his knee. "Hey Sam," he said. All I could think of was the milk I was about to receive.

Meanwhile, I sauntered over to the man as casually as possible. The man, Marge calls him Bill, has magic fingers, but it's not good to give humans too much power, so I waited a few seconds before I let myself purr under his touch.

The man and I became best friends, but the woman still wouldn't let me in the house. One day, three new people came to the house. A younger woman and two boys. The females left to go shopping, which left just us guys. By now, the man had moved a bed into the shed for me, because he used his wheelbarrow when it was warm, and I had a plastic fresh water dispenser out there, too. I think the woman bought it.

The man took the boys out on his boat, and just like always, I was waiting on the dock when the three of them came back from their ride around the lake.

"Boys, this is Sam," the man said. Boys. Humph. I didn't like that they had MY name, but I allowed them to pet me. They smelled like cat, which made them less suspicious.

"Grandpa, when did you get a cat?"

We all walked up to the house together and I went right inside with the three of them. The man always let me come inside when the woman was not at home. I liked it in there. It was cool and dark, even on hot days. Plus, the man gave me many delicious things from the fridge. Sardines and something called hummus and all sorts of treats.

"Sam likes hummus, Mom," one of the boys said after the ladies had come home and everyone was at the picnic table eating hot dogs. I had a hot dog too, without a bun. It was delicious.

"Did you let that cat in the house, Bill?" said the woman. I didn't care for her tone. I had a name. My name was Sam. I left the rest of my hot dog uneaten and walked with dignity to my shed to sulk.

Winter came, and she relented. She couldn't get me into their old cat carrier to take me to the vet; I was too big. Instead, the vet came to our house and told her I was about five or six and in very good health, but too fat.

The woman put the man and me on diets. We didn't like them. Whenever she left, he ate a candy bar while I snacked on kippers.

There were patches of sunshine in the house, where I would feel warm even in winter, but I felt warmest with my nose stuck inside the man's slipper. I could sleep and dream nice dreams like that.

Spring came and the man and I had our yard work to do. I took mouse patrol while he cut the grass and trimmed the shrubs. Then we'd sit on the picnic table together and have a snack. Salad and tuna if the woman was home; beer for him and cream for me if she was gone.

Sometime in the middle of the second or third summer, it occurred to me that I had stopped sitting on the hill every morning and evening. Why had I done that? I could hardly recall. Life was good, and, despite the lady not paying a lot of attention to me, continued in that way for many years.

One particularly fine spring day, the man hammered nails into a loose board on the dock and the woman filled her bird feeder. She didn't allow me to stalk anymore, and truth was, I'd grown too content to bother. I was standing by, on mouse patrol, though there'd been none of those for years, either, when I saw another cat.

The small female tabby rubbed against the woman's ankles, making her drop the plastic cup she used to fill the bird feeder.

"Toot," the woman said, looking down.

Just then, the man walked up.

"Who are you calling Toot?" he said, bending down to scratch the top of my head. "Did you forget this cat's name is Sam?"

"No," the woman said, in a much quieter tone than she usually talked. She looked down at the cat and then walked right through it. She opened the door and went into the house.

The man said, "She's finally losing it, Sam. Toot died long before you entered the picture."

That's when I realized that Toot was a ghost cat. Only I could see her. Toot meowed right in my face. I meowed back.

"That's okay, boy. Let's go see what's for lunch."

Toot didn't follow us in the house, but she was back outside the next day.

We discussed things and she gave me the story. She'd lived a long and happy life with the man and the woman and their children in another house for a very long time until she died.

I told Toot about my other family. I'd forgotten about them until that moment.

"So is this heaven?" I wondered. It couldn't be. The man and woman could see me.

"No," Toot confirmed. "This is real. Heaven is different."

"Oh," I said.

"Sam, what are you howling at?" The woman, back to her old cranky self, said, opening the door. "Get in here," she added.

"She was my special friend," Toot said, as I stepped toward the house. "Just like the man is yours."

The next day, Toot was there again.

"Why are you here?" I asked the little cat. No wonder the woman kept putting me on a diet. She wanted her dainty little thing back. "Are you haunting me?"

"No, Sam," Toot said.

"It's almost time for you to come with me. I didn't want you to be afraid, so I came to help you transition."

"Transition?"

"Die," Toot said matter-of-factly.

"I'm dying?"

"Yes, Sam. You have feline leukemia. It will be hard on the people, but they will be okay. I came to put the idea in Marge's head that you should go quickly, with me, and not suffer."

I had been feeling a little sore lately. It had been ages since I'd had an appetite, although I tried to eat with my old enthusiasm for the man's sake. I knew when she said it that Toot wasn't trying to scare me. She was telling me the truth.

"What's heaven like?"

"It's a jungle paradise, a kingdom of animals, with no hunger, no cold, no pain, no sleep, just endless hunts that end in sweet dances."

I felt sad, but knew it was the way of the world. All things must pass away. Still, I vowed to make my last days with the man special. I knew I had a place in his heart as large as the spot Toot held in the heart of Marge. Those places would always be here, even when I wasn't anymore.

So that night I slept by his side with my nose snuggled into his slipper and walked out with him the next morning to retrieve the newspaper. Later, we walked down to the dock where I waited for him to finish his boat ride. Before dinner, while he was napping in his room, I patrolled the house, wondering if Toot would come in finally to get me, or if I'd have to go out to the hill to meet her.

The woman sat on the sofa, looking out at the water. She had tears in her eyes. I had never seen that before. I jumped up on the sofa to comfort her. I'd never done that before, either.

"It's time, Sam," she said, and she petted me softly on the sides of my face, smoothing my whiskers. It was not the way I liked to be petted, but I let her do it, for Toot.

"I'm doing this while he's sleeping, because," Marge said, and started to cry. I dozed and when I woke, the vet in his white coat was with us. While the woman was crying, I slipped out of the house and went up the hill and waited there for Toot. I knew she would come.

Truth into Fiction

The bare bones of Sam's story are true. My mom imagined where he'd come from before my dad found him. She imagined his cat voice and his cat thoughts. She thought up Kitty Heaven. But the basic people parts are true. That's just one of the ways you can start with a true story and make it something entirely different.

Dialogue

After my mother read my typed version of her story, she called and said "You fixed my problem."

"What do you mean? I put the summary of your ending into scenes."

"But the reason I couldn't do that myself was because I didn't know how to write dialogue."

"Oh."

I hadn't even noticed that she'd stopped writing scenes and started summarizing at the point where Sam's people came more fully into the story. She had made Sam's voice so rich and distinct, it was easy for me to drop in and complete things in the same style.

Dialogue, the voices of the characters speaking, is different than, but related to, narrative voice. Each character needs a distinct vocabulary and verbal idiosyncrasies, but all of that is held together by the unified overarching narrative voice of Sam. We hear Marge and Bill the way Sam hears Marge and Bill. Or more accurately, the way the writer imagines Sam hearing Marge and Bill.

Writing realistic dialogue is difficult, but there are some tricks. First, cut out all the normal types of things people say when they first come into contact. All the "hi" and "how are you" and "fine" stuff. Dialogue should sound realistic, but not be realistic. Cut all the boring pauses, half-thoughts, "ums" and "likes." Or, use them to show character, but sparingly.

Some good uses of dialogue are to efficiently move plot forward, develop a character, or highlighting conflict: "Did you see the way that coward took off when he saw me get out of the car?"

One of the worst uses of dialogue is to tell backstory: "Hi Joe, I am your sister Becky, come back to see you after all these years."

When I write dialogue, I let myself think about how people really talk, how I might say something, or how a person I know who has qualities in common with the character I'm writing dialogue for might speak. I also love to listen to other people, their stories, the way they put sentences together. When I'm alone in a restaurant or the mall, I'll often eavesdrop. It's part of the job of a writer to pay attention to how people talk and then replicate the interesting bits as artfully but truthfully as possible in story.

Determining Reading Level

Children's literature is divided into several categories: picture books, nursery rhymes, biographies of historical characters, fictional chapter books, young adult fiction and memoir. The length of these stories varies widely, and there are differing guidelines depending on age and reading level of target readers.

Sam is fifth grade level "chapter book," meaning it has more words and fewer pictures. My children's lit scholar friend, Micki, tells me that *Sam* is a bit short for a chapter novel, and for the correct page length, Sam should have a few more chapters of fun adventures.

If you're writing a children's story, you'll need to know the age appropriate group. To determine reading levels in Microsoft Word:

1. Choose the Tools menu.
2. Select "spelling and grammar" option.
3. Select "show readability stats."
4. Click "OK."

After the spell and grammar check, a box will pop up with Flesch-Kincaid reading level statistics.

Exercise 21: Summary into Scene

High points of story should be scenes; less important moments can be summarized. Is there a particular place in your story where you summarized instead of dramatizing a fully fleshed out scene? Change it now, rewriting the summary into a scene. Let events unfold as if you're watching a movie in your mind, and write at least one section of dialogue.

Exercise 22: Your Voice

Recognizing Sam's voice is easy, because it's so distinct. But what about YOUR voice? How do you recognize it and why might that be helpful? Voice is what makes a piece of writing special, uniquely yours. Your narrative voice should sound natural. The voices of your story's narrator may or may not be your own. If the narrator is also a character in the story, as is usual in contemporary storytelling, the further the character is from who you are, the further the voice will be from your natural rhythms.

Many writers develop unique voices for every book. Others have a voice that is recognizably unique no matter how many stories they've told. What you want from your own voice is for it to keep the reader inside the vivid continuous dream of the story.

The exercise requires two pieces of writing: something by an author you admire, and something of your own. A page or a few paragraphs of each.

Read through the first paragraphs of the story you have chosen to imitate.

1. Copy the paragraphs into your notebook.
2. Now, directly under those paragraphs, rewrite the paragraphs in your own voice, with your own style, as you would write it. To do this, don't think about how many words the author used per sentence or any other technique. Think about what she was trying to say in that paragraph. Then say it, in your own words.
3. Copy the paragraphs of your own story into your notebook.
4. Rewrite your paragraphs in what you feel is the author's voice. Use all of his/her stylistic tics and ways of phrasing things.

Auster Example

Here's a short example of just one paragraph I rewrote from *Brooklyn Follies*) by one of my favorite authors, Paul Auster:

1. Auster's Paragraph

   "I finally hit upon an idea that Rachel would have approved of. It wasn't much of an idea, perhaps, but at least it was something, and if I stuck to it as rigorously and faithfully as I intended to, then I would have my project, the little hobbyhorse I'd been looking for to carry me away from the indolence of my soporific routine..."

2. 2. My rewrite of Auster:

   "So I got this idea that Rachel would like. It wasn't much but it was something. If I stuck to it, I'd have a little project, which is after all what I'd been looking for. Something, anything to take me away from the lazy dullness of my days."

3. Here's a longer example from my own work:

   "She didn't want to be here. She'd had fun at first, talking about poetry, making up quizzes, even grading was a power trip. But, little by little, problems mounted, beginning with the magic trick.

   She'd allowed a student to perform this trick, which entailed spilling a packet of non-dairy creamer to the floor, and, as it streamed downward, lighting the lowest, first fallen flakes with a hidden Bic, flicked so quickly she didn't have a chance to say "No fires in class!"

   The flame flared and died before she could even get upset. Like everyone else in the room she gasped in amazement at the fire that roared and died in the space of seconds. It was a very cool trick. Everything would have been fine had it not been for the smoke. And the fire alarm. And the gathering teachers outside her door culminating in the principal coming to investigate."

4. As Auster might revise:

She would rather be anywhere else on earth but this particular hellhole. At first it had been a lark, chatting about poetry, formulating quizzes, grading as if by the hand of God. The disasters accumulated incrementally, beginning with an inauspicious magic trick.

She'd granted the student's request to perform this trick, which seemed to involve nothing more than spilling out a restaurant-sized packet of non-dairy creamer. The acne-faced devil whipped a sturdy Bic from the pocket of his carefully torn jeans, lighting the falling powder from below.

The flame that roared up and vanished in the blink of an eye was rather breathtaking, and she might have let it go at that if the billowing smoke hadn't set the fire alarms to clanging, which naturally brought a cluster of concerned teachers, and the school's principal, to her door.

What I Learned

Voice is so much a part of who we are. In life, I'm often impatient; my writing reflects that. I saw right away, even as I was typing his paragraph, how our differences come out on the word/sentence level. He uses unusual words in interesting ways. I'm too impatient to wait for the perfect word, I use whatever pops into my head, and my vocabulary, it must be said, is not as impressive as his.

On the sentence level, and this is still just typing out his piece (which, when I practiced the exercise, I used more of than I included in this text, due to copyright issues) I noticed that he uses lots of long, complex, very elegant sentences. I admire these kinds of sentences, but I don't normally write them.

And then his dense paragraphs. I don't have the confidence he does with the long dense paragraphing. He seems assured that he can keep a reader's attention. I keep my paragraphs short; they sort of metaphorically wave their hands and tap dance and say "Hey, I'm interesting! Pay attention to me!" His paragraphs say "I'm smart, and erudite, and I know it. I'm a confident storyteller used to holding everyone in the room's breathless attention."

So I think there's a confidence in Auster that I lack. A confidence and sureness and a certain level of intelligent diction. At the same time, he's not pompous. He's funny and clever, too. It's such a dazzling act. I just didn't know quite HOW he pulled it off until I did this exercise.

And then when I tried to rewrite my original paragraphs in Auster's voice, it was harder than rewriting HIM in MY voice. Because again, I'm not about to linger and sweat over the sentences. So because I was doing it quickly, off the top of my head, it was really hard to imitate his wonderful voice with any authority, although I think I COULD do better if I really took the time.

There is a point in my writing when I DO take time to polish the sentences (that would be the final draft) but by then my syntax is already established so it would never come out quite Auster-like. Which is fine. I am who I am, voice and all. But at least now I know WHY.

Exercise 23: What Did You Learn?

What did you learn about your voice? Think, write and discuss.

Outstanding Children's Books & Authors

Ping: Marjorie Flack
Ferdinand the Bull: Munro Leaf
Headless Horseman Rides Again: Jack Prelutski
Sylvester and the Magic Pebble: William Steig
Shel Silverstein
Chris Van Alsberg

Comparative Fairy & Folk Tales

Petite Rouge: Mike Artell
Sam and the Tigers: Julius Lester
The Rough-Face Girl: Rafe Martin
Three Little Wolves and the Big Bad Pig: Eugene Trivizas
Rapunzel: Paul O. Zelinsky

SEVEN

Revision

"Use your intuition to determine what to save

and what to let go."

Sara Lewis

A Writer's Intuition

I once wrote a novel with a protagonist and antagonist who had the same goal: they both wanted the same piece of lake property and they both believed they deserved it. The protagonist wanted the lake property because she loved the water and wanted to start her own business renting the tiny cottages on the land to tourists. The antagonist wanted the property because she could make a quick buck flipping it for resale. The antagonist was not a monster, she was just greedy. And wounded.

At the climax of the story, the antagonist, who had never been violent to this point, pulled a gun on the protagonist. And then the protagonist disarmed the antagonist by doing some fancy karate moves, for which she had never shown the least inclination. As I read this section, I intuitively knew I'd violated character, twice.

In revision, I had two choices. I could have gone back and planted seeds, reworking my characters to develop these latent qualities, maybe have the protagonist work out every morning on the beach or break up a bar fight, or both. And the antagonist could go to the shooting range and with a steely look in her eyes, arms extended, her finger pulling the trigger of a big black gun, shooting hole after hole directly into the center of her target.

But my intuition chose the other thing, which was rethinking the climax to align better with my characters as they were written. I deleted the gun along with the karate moves. And my story felt more natural, less forced. Cops have gut instincts and writers have intuition. They're the same thing, really, and everyone on the planet is born with this inner knowing, instinctual understanding about what's right for them, and what's wrong. Most people don't pay close enough attention to their intuition, but writers need to develop this sense, especially as they read over their first drafts.

In my case, I knew my narrative needed conflict at the climax, but also that the way I wrote it felt false. Conflict needs to arise naturally from who the characters are and the way they react to whatever disaster, big or small, internal or external, that brings them to the climax of the story.

Revision Motivation

You've written the story. It's been told, which releases the immediate need to get it down on paper. Getting "side-tracked" or "discouraged" or "stuck" or just not knowing where to begin to revise are common writer dilemmas. If you want to make your story shine, schedule time every day to polish it.

Possibly, upon reading it over, the story isn't what you thought it would be. Mine always fall far short of the beautiful dream fully formed in my head before I begin typing. We all have ideas about what our stories will be before we write them. They're all planned out, so pretty in our minds.

It can be discouraging when our actual finished first draft doesn't reflect the brilliance of the original idea. But this happens all the time. A story is never as good on paper as it is in your head. That's just a fact of the writer's life. In revision, we try again (and again) to get it right.

Revision Example

Death of the Only Living Poet (Draft)

There were only four dry days in June the year my basement flooded. At first blissfully unaware of this event I watched the rain, dark and beautiful, pour thick like honey over my windows. I looked skeptically at the grey sky full of densely bunched clouds and let my eyes fall to the pavement that mirrored points of showy light from my neighbor's taillights as they backed cars from garages and headed for work.

My husband was out of town and thus I became frantic when I started down the steps to wash a load of laundry and discovered boxes, clothes, and assorted lawn furniture floating around in disheveled good humor. I called my Dad. Mother answered the phone.

"Alison, you sound frantic," she noted before passing the receiver to my Dad.

"Put on a pot of coffee. I'll be over in a minute. Your Mother wants to know are you pregnant yet?"

It was a family joke. I was on my second marriage and neither time did I "have to" get married. This seemed to astound my parents. As I was staring out the kitchen window during this exchange I replied that my belly wasn't growing yet but my grass sure was. It grew lush and dark green over my yard like an expensive rug. The little drops of rain could be scattered diamonds.

So Daddy relit the pilot light on my furnace and I don't know what all else. He instructed me to push the left over water t the drain (which he had unclogged) with a broom. We surveyed the soggy boxes, etc. that comprised the basement.

"Hadn't you finished unpacking yet?" Daddy wondered in an echo of my mother's tone.

"Yeah, sure, but this is just old stuff we don't know what to do with."

"Well I'd go through it if I were you. The boxes will mildew if you don't."

This is the sort of useful advice I had been getting from my parents since I'd married Mark, whom they adored because he took good care of me and had the sense to buy a house in the suburbs instead of renting rooms in a crash pad/commune. Not that that's exactly what my first husband and I had done, but this is the dichotomy my parent's attitude suggested.

For my part, I was living in a dream. A house, a car in excellent repair, credit cards, a diamond ring – Mark had made all of these things I had never had before available to me. I was not about to let one bit of mildew spoil my perfect world.

The first box I tried to open fell apart in my hands. My heart did a little skid when I saw my poems inside, the ink smeared, the paper limp with moisture.

"And so I don't know whether to just throw them all out, or go through them and try to salvage, or what," I was telling Mark that night when he called.

"Just toss them honey," was his sensible, shorthanded advice. And I was going to. But I couldn't, quite. I knew that part of myself, the poet, was gone. My compulsion to write had disappeared as mysteriously as it had arrived. I had expected to write poems forever but one had not crowded my thoughts or overtaken my pen in over a year. Before Mark and I were married. I missed the odd satisfaction and comfort of distilling my life in verse. But I didn't know how to tempt the muse back into my life.

I had first become aware of poetry when I was four and had swallowed a bottle of baby aspirins. This was not a babyish suicide attempt, but a case of mistaken identification. I had taken the little orange tabs for candy. Granny brought A Child's Garden of Verse into the children's ward and consoled me with rhyme as I sat in an unaccustomed diaper and hospital gown behind the high bars of a hospital crib. I remember my indignation and sense of helplessness as the nurse had diapered me and set me in the cage. Did she think I was an infant? Didn't she know I was a big sister and did not wear diapers or sleep in a crib anymore? But Granny's soft voice and her precious gift lulled me into a place where I was to forever feel comfortable – the world of words.

Poetry had nudged it's way into my life. Seventeen years later, it was gone. I had finally stopped expecting it to return.

"I guess that part of my life is over," I mused, wondering about that feeling – part compulsion, part inspiration – that caused me to rhyme. Sighing, I brought the soggy bunch of papers up the stairs and carefully laid them out about the house, on carpets and tables, on counters and beds, to dry. I had not written a poem since before my wedding, over a year ago. Still, I kept busy with my new house. I didn't work outside my home, but inside the toaster and coffee pot gleamed, the rugs stood brushed and the beds were always made. I had all the time in the world for my beloved novels. I'd even joined a book club.

By the oddest coincidence, the book I'd just finished was a novel whose protagonist was a woman poet. At the back of the book, a section of poetry had been inserted. I read the poems, amazed. Until that moment, I had believed Robert Louis Stevenson had had the last word, after Shakespeare, on poetry. But here was a live person, writing a sort of poem I had never even heard about (though later I found it was called confessional free verse) and it seemed to me that her lines spoke to and challenged me.

"A poet has to fall in love to write," said Jong, But that didn't seem true in my case. I was just so damn comfortable, so complacent. I pinched myself a lot on the way to the grocery store or the mall. I had everything except poetry.

I had discovered that I was far from being the only living poet. There was Erica Jong, and her contemporaries. I was in lofty company. But, even if I did want to write again, what would I say? Versifying my happiness seemed sentimental, almost as foolish as composing an ode to my polished refrigerator.

My other occupations, besides cleaning house, was shopping. I had been poor for so long that I was still amazed when I opened my closet and saw not the old Levi's and flannel shirts, not the one or two dresses culled from Goodwill, but rows of slacks, and sweaters, a blouses, and skirts, and slips, and housecoats, and jackets, and shoes, and boots...I had earrings to match all my outfits, handbags, hats ... baby doll nighties and penoirs. And I had books.

So after the pages had all dried, they naturally rippled and puckered into an unbearable mess.

"Mom, can I borrow your typewriter?" She told me to keep it as long as I needed it. I had it two or three years, and every time I mentioned it, she'd just ask how my writing was going and not to worry because she didn't use it any more. I of course typed and retyped and am in fact still revising some of my first fifty or sixty poems. The ones that survived.

As I began to type out the first drafts, though, after the flood, something good happened. Besides revision, I also discovered that I could woo inspiration, the old seductress would come again.

Major Overhaul

I changed this draft substantially from the final version you read in Chapter 3. Only the first and last lines remain the same. Sometimes, you have to start all over from scratch. Before I began to revise, I asked myself what the piece was about. I needed to be able to say it in one sentence:

This story is about a young woman who fell in love, lost her creative impulse, and found it again.

After I figured this out, I deleted everything not related to this idea. Then added drama through details that signify the importance of this pivotal moment in a young writer's life. Every time I added something, I asked myself if what I wrote spoke to the focus sentence. Next, I came up with a narrative sequence with more dramatic potent for a stronger structure.

Beginning: Falls in love. Middle: Loses creative drive. End: Finds it again.

I made one more big change. Even though my story was true, I mislabeled it as fiction, for no particular reason other than I was teaching myself to write, and at that time, everyone published thinly veiled accounts of their real experiences and called it fiction. But "Death of the Only Living Poet" is more accurately a memory piece, part of the creative memoir that runs through this text. It could even stand alone as a personal essay about an important step in my writing life.

Research

One of the first things I did after cutting all the extra stuff from the story was research the setting, suburban Michigan in 1977, for some popular cultural things going on that year that had significance in my own life. I used a search engine on the internet (I adore Google!) to look at music, movies, literature, television, and fashion. By simply typing in "1977 movies" and "1977 fashion" I was whisked back to the past, my memory jogged. You'll notice that a lot of what I researched, remembered, and wrote about before revising was added to my finished story.

1977 Pop Culture

Songs I loved:

"Dreams" by Fleetwood Mac

"Running on Empty" by Jackson Brown

"Blinded by the Light" by Manfred Mann

Other music stuff from '77:

Elvis died. August 16.

Disco (Saturday Night Fever) How Deep is Your Love

Movies I loved:

Star Wars

Annie Hall (academy award/best film)

A Novel:

How To Save Your Own Life by Erica Jong

Television I Watched:

Fantasy Island

Eight is Enough

Three's Company

Fashion I Wore:

Hot Pants (now known as short shorts)

Bell Bottoms (flared jeans, now known as boot cut)

Platform Heels (I think they still call these shoes platforms.)

Digging for Details

After I collected these details, I did quick free-writes to try to express what the details meant to me and how they might fit into my themes. Here's what my freewrite looked like. They are not polished prose, but exploratory writings.

Freewrites

I loved the song *Dreams* by Fleetwood Mac. I had long loved the blues band called Fleetwood Mac. It took me awhile to warm up to new singer Stevie Nicks, but this song did the trick.

Even though he was bloated and embarrassing by 1977, I cried when Elvis died on August 16. I cried for what he had meant to me. He had been my first love. When I was five, I used to sing along to his records in my bedroom. I stared at his picture on that first album cover for hours. I was surprised when he married Priscilla. I thought he'd wait for me.

Running on Empty by Jackson Brown. I loved this song, it hit some kind of deep unconscious chord for me, because I did feel empty without poetry.

Disco and *How Deep is Your Love?* by the BeeGees. I was in love with my husband, but I wondered if he loved me, who I really was, or just the idea of a perfect wife.

Blinded by the Light by Manfred Mann. I loved this song too. Music was so important to me then. I really thought with my marriage that I had finally seen the light. Turned out to be a little too bright.

Star Wars was the top film that year. We went to see this together and loved it. Before I married, I rarely went to movies. I didn't have the time, the inclination, or the money.

Annie Hall won an Academy Award for best film that year. I loved this movie, which is the story of a relationship from beginning to end—she leaves him finally in order to pursue her own dream. Prophetic in terms of my own path.

How To Save Your Own Life by Erica Jong is the book that made me think that there was poetry after marriage, that I was not the Only Living Poet. Between Annie leaving Alvy to pursue her dream and Isadora leaving her husband to fulfill hers, the seed had been planted.

Eight is Enough. I loved this cheesy family show. Before marriage, I hadn't even owned a television and would have thought it less than cool to watch a show like this. After marriage I felt safe enough to indulge my sentimental side. And I was ready for kids.

For dress up, I had a pair of black velvet hot pants, which I wore with cork-soled platform shoes. For casual, I always wore faded "bells." I was a hippie playing housewife, but I wanted so much to be a mom and have a perfect happy family like the sitcoms on television.

Setting and Subtext

The details of setting reveal character in subtextual ways. If you didn't get the subtext down on the first or second draft, now's the time to think about layering it in.

Details, props, and locations, need to be just right. This will happen naturally much of the time. But, as you read through your draft, if things don't feel true, if you're jerked out of the vivid continuous dream, if details are out of place or superfluous, take out whatever doesn't need to be there and replace it, only if necessary, with what does. Avoid meaningless clutter, unless clutter has meaning for your character.

Consider a car: is your character's car neat as a pin, all CDs in the case, maybe in alphabetical order, with a single bottle of water in the cup holder, no dust on the dashboard?

Or slightly messy with a couple of empty water bottles in the back seat next to a rolled up yoga mat and an unfolded map?

Or a sty: used fast food wrappers, empty beer cans, overflowing ashtray?

Our bookshelves, iPod playlists, laptop screensavers, bedrooms, the way we dress, all reveal subtle cues about who we are.

Exercise 24: Setting Subtext

What sits on your character's bookshelf? (Not necessarily book, but if they are books, what kinds? Comic books? *War & Peace*?) What songs are on the iPod play list? Or does she listen to podcasts? Describe laptop screensavers, things in her closet, whether she has photographs in her wallet or on her walls, and, if yes, then, how many and of who. What food does she keep in her refrigerator?

Revising Character

When writing for an audience, the key is to form a bond between reader and character. Readers empathize with protagonists when they feel the emotional weight of the character's plight. With this vital connection forged, readers will support a character's goals, feel the pain, and root for success.

One way to ensure this basic connection between reader and character is to put every scene in the point of view of the person with the most to lose. In a novel or screenplay, there may be several points of view. In a shorter piece, perhaps just one.

In order to figure out what's at stake, and who has what to lose, the writer must know her characters and every one of their deep, dark secrets. Spend time thinking and writing about character without having a final draft agenda. I used to want all my thoughts and certainly all my writing, to add up to pages. Now I know that when beginning a new story, it's better to write and think without being so focused on the final project. Now I understand I'll throw a lot of pages, and ideas, away. This thinking and writing without an end agenda is the key to breathing life into the figments of your imagination.

The most powerful way to get deep into your characters' head is to ask the same question (originally posed by Ron Carlson, I believe) three times. I don't know why this works, but it does.

1. What's your secret?
2. What's your real secret?
3. What's your REAL secret?

Here are my answers from "Death of the Only Living Poet."

1. I miss poetry.
2. I want to write again.
3. My marriage is smothering me.

Exercise 25: What's Your Secret?

Answer the three questions for your main character, or any character who eludes your sharpest depiction.

Character Subtext

Creating empathy between reader and character is subtle. Subtextual. When writers say something is too "on the nose" it means that what they're reading lacks subtlety, lacks subtext. The author has *told* not *shown*.

Telling instead of showing emotional content cheats readers. We like to bring our own intelligence and insight into the experience. It's WHY we read.

This is not an absolute rule, because there are no absolute rules, but important moments deserve fully-fleshed scenes, told in real time, through the point-of-view character's perspective. Lower key moments can be told through summarization, transition, reflection.

Let a character's actions demonstrate who they are. If your story is full of adverbs and other direct statements of active and emotional terrain, take most of it out and rework it with subtextual cues.

More subtle than saying "she lied" or "she said slyly" is to depict the body language or facial expressions that indicate subliminally that this person is a liar. Maybe she can't look the person she's lying to in the face. Maybe she absently touches her mouth. Maybe she looks up to the right instead of to the left. Maybe her face turns bright red when she lies, like my student who said she missed class the day papers were due because her grandmother died.

At the time, I thought her red face was due to other strong emotions: shyness, embarrassment, grief. And it's fine for readers or other characters to not get the liar right away. A gradual reveal is effective.

I found out my student had lied at the end of the semester, in a private conversation.

"This was a difficult semester for you, with your grandma dying," I said.

"She didn't actually die," my student said, blushing again. "But she was in the hospital. And she was really sick."

I was surprised that she admitted her lie, but it must have been haunting her, and she was trying to repair the wrong. Looking back, I can see that the red face indicated her discomfort with lying.

And that's what readers can do, too. They can look back and say, "Yes, the hints were there. I just didn't see them, but now it makes perfect sense."

Avoid being overly dramatic. Melodrama would have been my student bursting into tears and running out of the room when I mentioned her grandma dying. Sure, it happens in life. Terms like *high maintenance* and *drama queen* were invented for such people. And the term *stereotype* was invented for characters that can be boiled down so easily.

The deeper the emotion, the harder it is to be subtle, and the easier it is to slip into cliché. Eyes welling with tears, hearts breaking, filling, aching, beating fast, racing, all of these overused expressions lack positive impact, they don't make language memorable because it's not interesting language if a million other writers have written it before. A reader's eyes will glaze with too many of these modes of description. In revision, ruthlessly cut clichés.

And when in doubt, underplay strong emotion.

Ways to show anger: raised voice, red face, breaking a pencil or a dish, hitting, slapping, putting a fist through a wall, slamming a door, slamming a book shut, uttering an obscenity, shouting, giving the finger, lighting a cigarette, leaving the room, giving a partner the silent treatment.

Which is most original? Which fits YOUR character?

When I was a young hothead, my husband and I would get in an argument and I'd storm out, get in my car, and drive to the corner store for a pack of cigarettes. It didn't matter that I'd quit smoking years before. I always started puffing again when we had a major blow up. These days, we don't have big fights. On the rare occasion that we have words, I'll complain about him to my journal.

Those two types of responses are more real to me than a million dishes thrown against the wall.

Experts say 97% of all communication is non-verbal. Subtext reveals motivation and desire, and motivation and desire set up conflict.

Exercise 26: Subtle Emotion

Using less dialogue and more gesture, write an underplayed, highly emotional scene without resorting to the usual clichés.

Subplots

Characters are revealed through their relationships, which creates more characters for the writer. The main character will interact with friends, enemies, family. Every minor character with a somewhat important relationship to the protagonist needs history, motivation, personality, a distinct voice.

These characters are where the subplots come in. As you develop your minor characters, a few of them will flower before your eyes and develop their own conflicts, maybe conflicts that reinforce the main themes or conflicts of the protagonist.

However many plots you get revolving, if you're writing popular fiction, they should all fit together, at least loosely, by the end of the story. In literary fiction, just about anything goes.

Also, subplots start after the main plot, and finish before the central climax. Layering in subplots is an art in itself. Some writers like to plot out each story on it's own and then fit the subplots in where they'll have the best effect. I've heard of authors who write their last scene first, their first scene last. There's no one trick to it; every writer has to find their own way. Just because it's easier for me, I try to write chronologically, in the order that things happen.

EIGHT

Workshop

"The best writing is rewriting."
E.B. White

Friends and Flow

The time a workshop leader told me my language was "ugly" and my character was a bimbo-slut. The time a published author offered to read my manuscript and pass it along to her editor if it felt like a good fit and then later said "sorry" but my novel wasn't professional enough.

The time my critique partners both told me a revision I was proud of was still "not quite there."

Those are all true stories. So are these:

The time a famous author saw a scene I'd posted in an online workshop and sent a private two-word email: "fabulous scene." The time my editor told me I was the best writer on her staff. The time an agent called and said "I love your book." And then when she said, at lunch in Santa Monica, "I want to sign you."

The workshop leader who called my character a bimbo-slut was needlessly cruel. He could have said my character was hard to empathize with or needed more positive qualities. He could have softened the blow.

But my critique partners and the writing friend helped me by being straight. Writers learn to write better not just by writing more, but by learning where in their plots things fall apart. This is why, however painful, I value the workshop experience, and hope you will, too.

Mentally Preparing for Table Reads

We'll learn practice a table read by workshopping a critique of an early draft of my flood-of-poems story.

Notice I said "early draft" and not "first draft." First drafts are for your eyes alone and should be written freely, without an internal critic, without attention to grammar, diction, or the rules and guidelines of an assignment. Just write your story. Tell it as honest and true as you can, even if it's fiction. Wait a day, or at least a few hours before reading your story again, then answer the following questions, and revise your draft accordingly. These are the same questions we ask during workshop, and it will help your first critique being heaped with negatives if you take care of some of the problems before you bring your story to the table.

Revision Questions

1. Is the opening effective? Does it hook the reader? Does it ask a question?
2. Is the ending effective? Does it feel complete? Does it answer the story question?
3. Does the story have conflict? Is it internal or external or both? If it's one or the other, how might it be both?
4. Is the main character believable? Sympathetic? Does she have consistent character traits and an intriguing flaw? Does she have a clear goal or desire?

5. Is the antagonist true? Motivated? More than stereotype evil? Does his thwarting of the protagonist come from a real place?
6. Does the story have a dramatic progression? Increasing tension? Does the tension erupt in climax and dissolve in a satisfying conclusion?
7. Who narrates the story? Is the narration effective?
8. Does the level of diction detract from or enhance the story?
9. Is there anything in the story that feels out of place and can be removed without sacrificing the mood and main idea of the story?
10. Is the theme clear? Does it resonate for the reader?

Critique Etiquette

For the Writer:

Bruised egos are common. It's the nature of the gig. Writers are a sensitive bunch, but we need to be tough when it comes to hearing constructive criticism. Most published writers have had their share of rejection. More than talent or connections, writers need thick skin when it comes to their work.

If your work is being critiqued, try to not take negative comments about the piece personally. These are just people's opinions, including mine.

If you're feeling put-upon, mortified, vilified, etc, realize every writer feels more or less the same way when their work is under discussion. A false though popular perception is feeling that YOU alone have been singled out for overly harsh comments.

In my workshops, I strongly discourage hurtful comments and will stop a critique I feel is too nasty. I also encourage dissent among critiquers because I think it's helpful to the writer. If some folks love your sentence and others think it must be deleted forever, you can pretty much assume that the critique is a personal opinion due to literary taste.

If everyone agrees on a certain point, jot a note, then forget about it for a week. Next time you pick up your manuscript for revision, look it over with fresh eyes and then decide who was right. Reflection after time, when the wounds aren't so raw, is the way to most benefit from critiques. In the end, though, only you, as the writer, can make that call. And don't agonize, go with your gut.

The way I generally know when a comment is right is because the critiquer has pinpointed something that I had vague misgivings about going in, but decided to ignore in favor of just getting the piece done.

When people point out things that “must be fixed” I had no misgivings about, or worse, things I love that they just hate, I try to look at the opinion as objectively as possible. If my gut says the “correction” is not needed, I simply disregard and move on. With practice, most of the time, you’ll be able to tell which comments are useful and which are not almost right away.

There is no set amount or percentage of critique to use or lose. Sometimes a workshop will yield lots of good helpful suggestions that you know right away will sharpen your work. Other times, maybe one comment out of the half hour of discussion will resonate and the rest is useless.

The reason we critique is because that one comment can be gold. It can take a piece of writing from just okay to wonderful. It’s why we’re here in the first place, to grow as writers.

There is a particular kind of writer who masks insecurity with ego. This writer’s body language clearly states that she has no intention of listening to anyone else’s opinion about their story, including mine. If you believe you have nothing to learn from your facilitator or fellow writers, it’s better to pretend otherwise, because an attitude of superiority often hides a supreme lack of confidence.

Another type of writer, whether from arrogance or insecurity, apologizes for her work by prefacing it with disclaimers such as “this is really rough” and “I didn’t have time." Bringing a "really rough" piece to a workshop implies a couple of things, neither good. One, that the writer had better things to do with the time than the rest of us, and therefore should be excused from completing a decent draft for the workshop. Two, it additionally implies that the writer could certainly do so much better, probably better than the rest of us, if they only "had the time." So don't apologize.

Nor should the writer being critiqued offer any kind of defense or explanation for any part of their work. If the writer being critiqued needs to preface a reading with a few brief facts the group needs to know, that's fine, but keep it short. A story should stand alone.

Every critique is basically saying "this worked for me" or "this didn't." Explaining what you were trying to do may soothe your ego for the moment, but it doesn't change the fact that for this critiquer, this bit did/did not work.

For the Reader:

Start with what you like about the story. Be specific. As the writer reads, circle or underline words and phrases that you want to go back to after the reading is complete. There will be time after the reading to formulate your thoughts as to what specifically you liked and why. Saying what you like about a story, spending some time being specific, and not just repeating what others have said, goes a long way in making the workshop an enjoyable experience.

Don't bother discussing grammar, spelling, or usage. It goes without saying that all of the above should be impeccable. If it's not, I'll let the writer know and work with them to fix it.

Circle the main character's name and continually try to figure out their goal/motivation as you read along with the writer. Goal and motivation are not generally stated within the text, but inferred through action, dialogue, and details. Your understanding of the character's goal might not be what the writer intended. That's fine.

You'll be handing back the copy of the story to the writer, so make sure you sign your name to the top of the first page, for the writer's information.

Give the story your deep attention. "I liked it" is not a good enough response, and I'll be asking you to elaborate.

If you ask a writer to expand on a character or to be more descriptive, it's always helpful to explain why. What information did you need to know about that character that was not given? What about more description would help the story feel real?

Spontaneous is good. I like to hear from everyone, and Round Robin ensures that, but it's particularly great when two critiquers disagree about some aspect of the story. And that includes me. If I say, "John should not be wearing a hat. It doesn't fit his character," it is perfectly acceptable for another class member to pipe up, out of turn, and say "I loved the hat! The hat must stay!" Two or three opinions are enough ; we don't need consensus from the whole group or a debate about who's right. What we like about story is often subjective, and it's good enough that the writer knows opinions are mixed.

Be tactful but honest, supportive of the work in general, and always, always, start with what you liked about the piece.

Exercise 27: Model Table Read with DRAFT of *Death of the Only Living Poet*.

NINE

Publishing

"Publish or perish."

Marshall McLuhan

About a Blog

A funny thing happened when I started a blog. I felt published. It was like a miracle. Characters have desires that drive them, but people do, too, and for many writers, the desire to be published supersedes everything else. I was a writer like that. It didn't matter that I'd been published in magazines. I wanted a book with my name on it. A book of poems, or short stories, or a novel. I didn't care, as long as it was a book.

Then the internet came along and changed my mind. I have my son, Mike Jablonski, to thank for suggesting I start a blog. He said he'd set everything up and write all the code. All I had to do was come up with content. Six years later, I'm still posting almost daily entries on "A Writer's Diary" at **www.cynthiaharrison.com**.

Exercise 28: Write a Blog

You, or one of your characters, decides to write a blog. What will you name it? Write the first entry.

Successful Self-Publishing

Traditional publishers, the kind that pay advances and royalties, are tough to approach without an agent. Slush piles of unsolicited manuscripts sometimes sit for years unopened. If you simply want 50 copies of your memoir for family and friends by Christmas, there are other ways to get a book into print.

I hired a friend with desktop publishing capabilities to print a limited edition of my fantasy, *Octoberland.* She designed a logo, and book cover with a photograph another friend gave me, and I was set to go. I didn't buy an ISBN number or a bar code, because this a privately printed, one-shot gift item that I wasn't planning to sell or distribute.

However, anyone can set up their own small press, find a printer, and pay to publish their own work. Virginia Woolf and Walt Whitman did it, and many now successful authors were first self-published. I did it with this book, and while I won't lie and say it was easy, reference books like Dan Poyneter's *Self-Publishing Manual* helped me walk through the complex steps involved in self-publishing.

If you don't want to do the work yourself, and I have to say, it's a LOT of work, many solid internet publishers are out there, ready and willing to print your book on demand, make it available in e-format, or run a small print order, for a reasonable cost to the writer. They then earn less money from sales than do traditional publishers.

Beware, however, of the so-called vanity presses, which charge too much money and deliver little except boxes of books to your door. They give no editorial advice and what you type on your computer screen is what you see in print, misspellings and all. Research any publishing company before signing a contract.

E-books

One of the problems with even a respected electronic publisher is that most often these titles won't show up in brick-and-mortar outlets unless you pay for distribution yourself, which can be costly.

Becky Reed's compelling, gritty memoir about overcoming compulsive emotional overeating, *Crumbs,* debuted through a self-publishing partnership with Amazon.com's BookSurge. Becky recommends writers who want to self-publish visit websites like Moira Allen's *Writing World* and *Lulu.com.* Becky notes that, "Lulu also has forums where people with questions can get answers."

Becky liked BookSurge's way of getting the books out to the public. "Amazon.com owns them, they are easy to work with, and have a good name in the publishing industry. Agents and traditional publishers respect them, which is important in case your book gets picked up down the road by a big name publisher. My books are available via many online outlets: Amazon, Borders, Alibris, Target, Walmart, and Baker & Taylor."

Start up costs, varying publishing packages, and other mystifying options all carry different price tags. Since she "already had experience with formatting, editing and graphic design" Becky chose BookSurge's $99 package. That price, at the time her book was printed, included "an ISBN, a color cover, black and white interior, as well as other little perks. They have a Talent Acquisition Program, which is a list that goes out to all the big name publishers. For more money, they will format, edit, create a cover, and do everything a traditional publishing house offers, including some marketing."

I once reviewed eBooks for RT BOOKclub, and while there were some exceptions, most of them were terrible, with standards well below what you'd see in a traditionally published novel.

Becky remarks that "Self-published books have a bad rap in the publishing industry, mainly because of the poor quality of the writing. An author can read and re-read, revise and revise again, but will always miss something that could have been changed to improve the work. It's good to have a new set of eyes examine your work, not only for typos, but to offer a fresh perspective one might not have seen before."

Traditional Publishing

If you decide to find an agent or approach traditional publishing house editors, specific names and addresses are listed in *Writer's Market* or *Literary Marketplace*, both available in libraries. If contacting a publisher, always send your query to a particular editor.

Finding an agent to submit your work for speeds the process. If you meet the agent or editor in person, perhaps at a conference, you'll need a verbal pitch. If you contact them by mail, the proposal package includes a query and sometimes a synopsis and the first 30-50 pages.

Fiction publishers and literary agents representing fiction insist that before querying, the author must have a completed manuscript.

The Pitch

A pitch is a catchy, short blurb that answers the question "What's your book about?" To get started on crafting a pitch, answer these questions:

Who is your protagonist?

What does she want?

Why?

What's the conflict?

Who's the antagonist?

After you've answered these questions, craft an elegant, flowing, interesting, one or two sentence pitch. Here's a model from my novel *Remodeling Eden*:

> Divorced Eve Delacroix has a tight budget and two months until tourist season to turn six dilapidated hunting cabins into shabby chic cottages. Jane, an ambitious realtor, wants the property, too, and she's not afraid of ruining Eve's life to get it.

Exercise 29: Write a Pitch

Write a pitch for the story you already wrote or put an idea for a new piece into pitch form.

The Synopsis

A synopsis, or outline in sentence form, (not a casual chain, although if you have one, it can help write the synopsis) explains the major events in your story, including any twists and how things end. Never say: "If you want to know how this ends, you'll have to buy my book..." Editors and agents universally despise this approach. In addition to giving the gist of your story, a synopsis should be impeccably written and use the voice of your story. Look up my synopsis model (of *Remodeling Eden*) is in Chapter 6: Genre if you need an example, but don't worry if yours is shorter. One page is fine. You have a 3-20 page story to work with; mine was 300 pages.

Exercise 30: Write a Synopsis

Write a synopsis for the story you already wrote, or for an idea you have for a new project.

The Query

A query is simply a one page letter with three concise single-spaced paragraphs. One way to structure a query is to start with an intriguing opening that somehow highlights your connection to the agent or editor. Biographical information, writing credentials or relevant experience often conclude the letter. A paragraph or two of summary that begins with a strong hook, often your pitch, fills the middle.

Always include a stamped, self-addressed envelope with your query or proposal package.

Model Query

March 21, 2006

Editor or Agent Name & Title
Publisher or Agency Name
Address

Dear Ms. X,

My feature article about Jennifer Crusie and Bob Mayer's collaboration will appear in May 2006 RT BOOKclub. It's not the first time I've published a piece about Crusie's work. I admire her distinctive voice and have worked to hone one of my own, most recently in my 90,000 word women's fiction manuscript.

In *Remodeling Eden*, Eve Delacroix has a tight budget and two months until tourist season to turn six dilapidated hunting cabins into shabby chic cottages. Newly divorced, she's undertaking another major renovation: her life. Jane is the ambitious Realtor who sold Eve the property. Now she wants it back, and she's not afraid of fighting dirty to get it.

In addition to reviewing over 500 novels in the past several years, I have published short stories and poetry in literary journals. Would you be interested in looking at chapters or the completed manuscript of *Remodeling Eden*?

Sincerely,

Cynthia Harrison
Address
Phone
email

Exercise 31: Query

Write a query letter. Use my structure, or get creative. No need to research who to send it to yet.

The Cover Letter

If an agent or editor responds to your query with a request to see the complete manuscript, send it as soon as possible, with a cover letter reminding them of their interest and restating your pitch.

Model Cover Letter

Date
Title
Address

Dear Ms. X,

I was happy to receive your letter asking to see the proposal for my women's fiction manuscript, *Remodeling Eden*. The main character, Eve Delacroix, is determined to turn six dilapidated hunting cabins into shabby chic cottages.

I'm a reader as well as a writer, and have long admired the humorous women-centered stories of Jennifer Crusie, Susan Elizabeth Phillips and Mary Kay Andrews. *Remodeling Eden* seeks to embody a similar sensibility.

I look forward to hearing your thoughts about *Remodeling Eden*. Along with the proposal, I'm enclosing a copy of my recently published feature on Jennifer Crusie and her new writing partner for RT BOOKclub.

Sincerely,

Researching Publishers

The most important thing an aspiring writer can do is to read widely in the genre they wish to pursue. Check who publishes your favorite stories. This is your target publisher. Many times, authors thank their own editors and agents on a dedication or acknowledgement page.

After researching to determine if your target agent or publisher accepts new clients, send proposals only to those editors and agents looking for new writers. Some will want a full proposal, some only a query. Some want the proposal by e-mail, others insist on regular post.

A wealth of publisher, editor, and agent information can be found on the internet as well as in *Writer's Market* and *Literary Marketplace.* Editors at publishing houses like writers to have agents; many won't look at unagented material. Agents don't often take chances on unpublished writers, which is why your manuscript has to sell itself.

Editors don't often accept unagented manuscripts, but most still read unsolicited queries. Querying FIRST means that if the editor or agent likes your query and asks to see material (usually a synopsis and three chapters) you are out of the slush pile. Write "requested material" on the outer envelope, which ensures escape from the dreaded slush pile.

Publishers are impressed when writers know the business, are familiar with the house imprints (six corporations own hundreds of publisher imprints) and authors, and can speak intelligently about how they see their work placed in the market. Know the names of successfully published authors who write things similar to your work. Don't say you're better than Stephen King or that you'll sell a million for them overnight, but do indicate, by your query or proposal, that you know your craft.

A few final pieces of crucial advice that can't be restated often enough: Never address a query to "Dear Agent" or "Dear Editor." Know the name and title of the person you're contacting, who their clients are, what kind of work they're looking for, and how they like submissions presented. That everything should be grammatically correct and sparkle with your best writing shouldn't have to be said, but I'll say it anyway, because I once had a student forward me an email from a publisher who said I was a terrible teacher for not telling her she had issues with grammar. Of course I'd told her, several times. She just didn't believe me, or maybe she wasn't listening.

Book Publishers: Selected List

Publishing is a huge industry, changing every day. Imprints and houses are bought and sold and, sometimes, vanish. Agents become editors, editors become publishers, publicists become agents. The rotating list of career titles turns in a constant, dizzying circle.

Currently, these are some of the imprints that fall under each of the major six publishing groups:

Hachette Book Group

Little, Brown
5-Spot
Center Street

HarperCollins Publishers

HarperCollins
Harper Perennial
William Morrow
Ecco
Avon

Holtzbrinck Publishers

Farrar, Straus and Giroux
St. Martin's Press
Picador
Henry Holt
Farber and Farber
Owl Books
Tor Books

Penguin Group

Dutton
Penguin
The Penguin Press
Riverhead
Jeremy P. Tarcher
Viking
G.P. Putnam's Sons
Berkley
New American Library
Onyx
Plume
Signet

Random House

Vintage
Doubleday
Knopf
Ballantine
Dial
Pantheon
Random House
Nan A. Talese
Villard
Crown
Delacourt
Dell
Del Rey
Fawcett
Ivy
Three Rivers

Simon & Schuster, Inc.

Scribner
Free Press
Atria
Simon& Schuster
Downtown Press
Pocket Books
Touchstone

. I've listed only the imprints I'm familiar with, and have not included children's, Christian, or other niche imprints I've never read. Fair warning: things could change tomorrow. Your best bet is to read widely and garner your own list of favorite publishers and imprints.

TEN

Film

"When the student is ready, the teacher appears."

Zen Proverb

Hollywood Finale

Back in Los Angeles, where I started this book, I told my agent about a friend of mine who wanted to write a screenplay together. My friend has a relative who's a big shot with one of the networks.

"Go for it," Mary Louise said, adding that the first step should be a pitch. Hollywood loves writers to pitch first, in person if possible. They're always having meetings and things, just like on *Entourage.*

Back in Michigan, I told my friend what my agent had said. My friend didn't want to pitch. She wanted to write something. Actually, she didn't want to write, she just wanted to tell me her story idea and then I could write it, if I wanted to.

So I called my agent and she said not to write a script yet, to just write a treatment, which is what they called synopses in Hollywood. That's the way it works, she said. They want the idea first, a little bit about the characters and plot, then, if that works, maybe they'll look at a script.

Being the person I am, I tried to please both agent and friend. After an afternoon of talking out the story with my friend, I gave myself a weekend to write a scene and a treatment. I knew the chances were good that none of this was ever going anywhere. But I had a lot of fun writing, and I thought I did a good job, so passed my work on to my friend and I told her she could show what I'd done to her relative in television or she could work on it some more herself.

There's been no word, so I'm assuming she stuck it in a drawer and forgot about it.

Moving to L.A.

Lee Goldberg says if you want to write for the movies or television, you should probably live close to Los Angeles, because of the pitch meetings, and also, when you get hired to write a show, you go to the studio every day and write with a group of collaborators just like Rob, Buddy, and Sally did on *The Dick Van Dyke Show.*

What Scenes Should Do

Movie scenes are image and dialogue based. According to Linda Seger, a great film scene should do four things: advance the story (perhaps through dialogue), reveal character (maybe by action), build an image (possibly using background visuals), and explore an idea (using all three).

Script Format

Setting up a script is totally different than formatting a fiction manuscript. There's software you can buy that will auto-format, but since I only wrote two scenes, and one of them is really short, I just did it by hand. The name of whatever character is speaking is centered and in caps. Dialogue lines are indented under that. For a first script, keep description to a bare minimum. Actors and directors like to add their own layers to your words. Images are fine, just don't go on for pages, or even paragraphs. And the images are not indented.

The first time a character is referred to, their name appears in all caps. Also, each scene starts with an all cap summary of location. EXT. means "exterior" and INT. means "interior." I found all this out on Wikipedia. Those guys know everything.

Model Script

<u>The Absolution of Gwen</u>

By Connie Haddad & Cynthia Harrison

EXT. CEMETERY – SUMMER DAY

A casket rests on a fresh grave.

MAN'S VOICE

Turn out the lights.

GWEN

Husband, father, does it mater that I can't remember which one used to follow me room to room, saying that?

A few dozen mourners stand on either side of the casket under a canopy, including ELAINE and LINDA.

ELAINE (THINKS)

She's here. I feel—is that her?

Elaine catches sight of a woman in a white cloak who seems to melt into a tree.

LINDA (THINKS)

Why would she kill herself?

Looks at Gwen's husband GARY.

Too obvious.

INT. RESTAURANT/BAR - AFTER FUNERAL

Linda and Elaine, standing at bar with their backs to it, look at the crowd of mourners, faces full, plates empty. Many are still drinking, some eat cake, some even laugh. Linda and Elaine hold almost empty glasses of wine.

LINDA

You pay for all this?

ELAINE

It's nothing.

Elaine turns to the bar and sets her empty glass on a napkin with the word INFERNO printed on it. The bartender approaches holding an open bottle of wine. Linda senses his approach, and turns to hold her glass toward him. He fills both wine glasses. The women keep their backs to the room.

LINDA

Why'd she do it?

Elaine drains her glass of wine and opens her purse. She pulls out her cell phone and clicks through the menu until she finds what she wants. She hands it to Linda.

ELAINE

You know Ollie, at the church? He's in my photography class. He took this. I think it's Gwen.

LINDA

Looks at the phone photo of a woman in a mask, holding a whip. Flips the cell closed and pushes it back toward Elaine.

This the same class Gwen was taking with you on Monday and Wednesday nights?

ELAINE

Gwen hasn't taken a photography class with me in ten years. She told me she was going to your new yoga thingy Monday and Wednesday nights.

She returns the cell phone to her purse.

Ollie was flashing this and a whole group of similar shots around the room. I got off a quick snap before he saw me. They work together, but I mean, he's...

LINDA

Last Man On Earth.

ELAINE

He's a maintenance man, for Chissakes. It can't be her. She's the best Catholic I know.

LINDA

Yes, even excommunicated.

ELAINE

So I'm crazy, right? The church secretary would not be posing like this for the handyman.

LINDA

It's her. I recognize the whip.

Gary, Gwen's husband, approaches Elaine. The room has cleared and BRAD, Gwen and Gary's teenaged son, leaves the restaurant jangling car keys.

GARY

Reaching out to embrace Elaine.

I cannot thank you and Dave enough for all this.

ELAINE

We wanted to. I'll call you tomorrow.

Gary hugs Linda, who pats him on the back, and carefully sets him away before he falls asleep in her arms.

LINDA

You gonna be okay?

GARY

Gotta be. For Brad.

He turns and walks out after his son.

ELAINE

Wouldn't it be ironic if Gary finally rejoins to human race now that Gwen is gone?

LINDA

I hope Brad's driving. Did you see how messed up Gary's eyes were? Gwen probably got those Secondals she used to do it from his stash.

Elaine looks toward the bartender, who is discreetly washing glasses a few feet away. Without glancing at her, he opens a fresh bottle of wine and sets it down between the women.

ELAINE

That will be it. Thank you.

She hands him a credit card.

What's this about the whip?

LINDA

I'm wondering if Ollie and those pictures is why Gwen killed herself.

ELAINE

You said you recognized the whip.

The bartender returns with the charge slip. Elaine signs it and pushes it across the bar.

LINDA

A week or so ago, Gwen invited me over for lunch. Brad and Gary were at a ball game.

ELAINE

She invited me, too. I was doing a shoot at the Arboretum.

LINDA

Yeah, she said. Anyway, when I got there, she'd just ripped a bag of salad open and was pouring it into bowls. She asked me to get the croutons from the pantry. I opened it and there was the whip. Same one. Braided leather, silver studs on the ends.

Linda picks up the bottle, pours the last two glasses out for them. They drink.

ELAINE

Will you go to the church with me tomorrow?

LINDA

As long as we're going to kick Ollie's ass or steal some pictures or something. I haven't prayed in twenty years and I'm not starting now.

**

Final Advice

Many of my students want to write screenplays and television pilots, but I suggest that after you move to California, you do what my agent suggested and write the treatment first. Use the same format as my synopsis model in Chapter Five.

Then hone your pitch until it sounds natural and hunt all over L.A. for people to tell it to. You do this by networking, joining groups, making phone calls, mailing queries. Don't pitch to a producer in a public restroom, interrupt an agent in a restaurant, or accost an actor on the street. Save the actual pitch for a proper business meeting or maybe a party if the timing seems right, like, say, you're in a conversation with a nice director who asks what you're working on.

Good Luck!

With Gratitude

This book got written with the help of so many wonderful friends and teachers.

Debbie Buczkowski and Debbie Bressman used their creative design and photography talents to come up with a lovely cover for the book. Debbie Buczkowski's technical expertise got me through the pre-printing stages of the publishing process.

My mom, Marjorie Hines, allowed me to use her children's story "Sam" in Chapter Six. And without my dad, William Hines, the real Sam would never have entered and enriched our lives.

Connie Haddad, Debbie Bressman, and Chuck Bressman contributed ideas to the screenplay scene in Chapter Nine. I just wrote them down.

Beth Trembley, Kris D'Arcy and Micki Schichtel read early drafts. Beth's notes on structure and one crucial addition, Kris's impeccable grammar and instinct for cutting excess, and Micki's expertise with children's literature all made this a much better book than it was before their edits.

Becky Reed graciously allowed me to quote and summarize from our interview at www.cynthiaharrison.com about her self-publishing experience, greatly improving the quality of information in Chapter Nine.

And finally, I wouldn't have had any text to write had it not been for my teachers. Jennifer Crusie (www.jennycrusie.com) taught me how to plot with conflict, Sara Lewis (www.saralewis.com) gave me intuitive writing lessons, and Barbara Samuel (www.barbarasamuel.com) showed me how to access my truest voice.

Creative Writing Authors & Texts

My fiction and creative non-fiction writing practices were also inspired by these writers and texts:

Paul Auster: *The Red Notebook*

Roland Barthes: *The Pleasure of the Text*

Charles Baxter: *Burning Down the House*

Elizabeth Berg: *Escaping into the Open*

Anne Bernays and Pamela Painter: *What If?*

Dorothea Brande: *Becoming a Writer*

Julia Cameron: *The Artist's Way* & *Floor Sample*

Raymond Carver: *Fires*

Rosemary Daniell: *Secrets of the Zona Rosa*

Annie Dillard: *The Writing Life*

Arielle Eckstut/David Henry Sterry: *Putting Your Passion Into Print*

Bonnie Friedman: *Writing Past Dark*

Elizabeth George: *Write Away*

Ellen Gilchrist: *The Writing Life*

Natalie Goldberg: *Writing Down the Bones*

Lee Goldberg & William Rabkin: Successful Television Writing

Gotham Writers' Workshop: *Writing Fiction*

Susan Carol Hauser: *You Can Write a Memoir*

Judson Jerome: *The Poet & The Poem*

Stephen King: *On Writing*

Brian Kiteley: *The 3 a.m. Epiphany*

Anne Lamotte: *Bird by Bird*

Noah Lukeman: *The First Five Pages*

Carole Maso: *Break Every Rule*

Robert McKee: *Story*

Judy Reeves: *Writer's Retreat*

May Sarton: *Journal of a Solitude*

Victoria Lynn Schmidt: *Story Structure Architect*

Charles Schulz: *Snoopy's Guide to the Writing Life*

Carolyn See: *Making a Literary Life*

Linda Seger: *Making a Good Script Great* & *Creating Unforgettable Characters*

Jane Smiley: *13 Ways of Looking at the Novel*

Christopher Vogler: *The Writer's Journey*

Virginia Woolf: *A Writer's Diary* & *A Room of One's Own*